D0716660

Behaviour Recovery

Behaviour Recovery

Recovery

A whole-school program for mainstream schools

Bill Rogers

LONGMAN

First published 1994
by the Australian Council for Educational Research Ltd
19 Prospect Hill Road, Camberwell, Melbourne, Victoria, 3124 Australia

First Published in Great Britain 1994 by
Longman Information & Reference
Longman Group Limited,
Westgate House, The High,
Harlow, Essex CM20 1YR, UK
Tel: (0279) 442601
Fax: (0279) 444501

Edited by Brigid James, Writers Reign
Designed by Tom Kurema
Illustrations by Bill Rogers and Elizabeth Rogers
Cover illustration by Sarah Rogers
Cover design by Tom Kurema

A catalogue record for this book is available from the British Library.

ISBN 0-582-26428-6

Printed in Great Britain at Quorn Litho, Leicestershire

Acknowledgements

I would like to acknowledge and thank all the teachers who have worked with me on developing the ideas relevant to behaviour recovery. They struggle daily to teach behaviourally disordered children to recover behaviours that many children seem to exercise with social ease.

These teachers have taught me a lot about how to work more successfully with behaviourally disordered children. Some of their experiences with behaviour recovery are shared in this book. Few people have original ideas; I don't. I've read widely, discussed widely, and utilised the approaches in this book with my colleagues and found these to be a very helpful way of teaching behaviour. I have appreciated, too, the many schools who have allowed me to work there as a consultant, and the children who have experienced successful changes in their behaviour at school.

Jenni, thanks once again for your patient typing (and your translation skills!). ACER have, as always, been consistently supportive of the project. My thanks to Ian Fraser, John King and Barbara Burton. I have been fortunate, once again, to have in Brigid James a supportive and ever patient editor. A big ta.

A number of people kindly reviewed the drafts of this book but my special thanks go to Janet Sainsbury and Marg Riley who encouraged me to go for it! Colleague support in practice.

Our oldest daughter contributed artwork to the text — many thanks Elizabeth. Our youngest daughter, Sarah, often came into my office during the writing of this book and was particularly intrigued with the drawings asking, 'Why do these children need them?' She often drew alongside me, to complement my efforts. Thanks to my supportive family for their patience and understanding.

Bill Rogers, Melbourne.

The He/She issue

The reason I've opted for 'he' as the preferred usage in pronouns is simply because it is the most commonly referred gender in terms of disruptive behaviour. Serfontein (1990) notes, with regard to ADD behaviours (attention-deficit disorder), that it is a disorder most commonly affecting boys (up to 20 per cent of male children).

I've also tended to use 'she' when referring to teachers because kindergarten and early primary school teachers generally tend to be female.

Bill Rogers

Contents

Introduction

I received a letter from a Year 2 teacher (seven-year-olds) about a little boy she described like this.

> ... being so out of balance that he spins off into chaotic turmoil constantly ... (he) is a blond-haired, blue-eyed ... freckly-nosed little boy with wing-nut ears ... his blue eyes are very expressive and you can usually predict his mood quite easily by just looking at him. His (attention-seeking) behaviours are too numerous to mention all of them but I'll list a few just to give you an idea.
>
> Instead of joining whole-class sessions on the mat, (he) goes down on all fours, finds top gear and goes for it; racing around the room, under and over the furniture, kicking his legs out (to catch furniture and make a noise). He comes back to the mat, briefly, to catch his breath — and off he goes again.
>
> He enjoys being an exhibitionist: he stands on top of the table with his pants around his ankles and does a little lower body shake. He breezed into the room one morning with the announcement 'I had baked beans for breakfast' and proceeded to flatulate, loudly. He also breaks wind and burps and makes any noise that he thinks will gain attention at the most opportune times (and the most inopportune time for the teacher). He is also a compulsive thief (money only) and a liar. He has great difficulty being responsible for his actions. Towards other children he is equally attention-seeking with pinches, punches, pulling hair, scribbling on or ripping up work etc.
>
> But for all this there is a lovable kid inside. I'm quite fond of Matt despite his behaviour. The real kid is very bright and has a quick wit and sense of humour. Unfortunately his home life provides little or no sense of security. His father is on medication for manic depression and his mother feels she just can't cope and will often walk out on them. She is, however, receiving guidance and that helps a bit. Sometimes they (the children) do

not have any lunch. The brother and sister are older but they also have huge problems.

Matt is typical of many behaviourally disordered (BD) students in primary schools. Many teachers can recount numerous stories like this one. Unlike children with physical disabilities these children get little extra teacher assistance or support services. When education resources are stretched, more and more is expected of the classroom teacher in terms of behaviour management, discipline and welfare provision.

Behaviourally disordered children are particularly frustrating for teachers and those outside the profession have little idea how draining these children are in terms of day-to-day management. If you are a primary school teacher no doubt you've come across children like Matt. While these children clearly have a right to learn and a right to schooling in a mainstream setting, their behaviour creates more stress than any other handicapping condition.

Helen (Matt's teacher) was able to work successfully with Matt to the point where '*he now sits attentively on the mat, raises his hand, and is quite a popular member of the classroom . . . his self-esteem is excellent. I can't change his home environment but he has felt safe at school . . .*'

What Helen did, as many other teachers whose stories are recounted here did, was to acknowledge the real difficulties at home but not let that stop her believing she could help Matt *learn* new behaviours in the school context. Using a combination of simple behaviour modelling, utilising the support of the other children (through classroom meetings), applying positive discipline principles, behaviour recovery principles and colleague support, Helen saw productive behavioural change in Matt. She notes, at the end of her letter, the impact of Matt on her life. '*Needless to say Matt will live in my memory forever.*' (Helen's program is outlined later in the book.)

Andrew is in Year 1, one of a class of thirty-one children. He stands out by virtue of his loudness, his restless wandering, his seat-rocking and his time off-task, (he's easily distracted and seems to be frequently inattentive). At his table even his 'normal' talking is loud. When he's on the mat during instructional time he squirms, rolls and grunts. Behaviourally disordered — of course. Difficult home life — no doubt. Frustrating to his teacher — naturally!

I worked with Andrew (and his teacher) to help Andrew modify his behaviour. Working on the assumption that a child has to learn to control his own behaviour we set out to teach him the alternative behaviours to loudness, seat-leaning, wandering etc. Rather than just punish him for these behaviours we taught him new behaviours. The grade teacher was given short time-release sessions from his class to literally *teach* Andrew how to sit (four-on-the-floor) and how to keep noise level reasonable. The teacher modelled loud conversation noise and then showed what reasonable conversation noise was and asked him to copy (rehearsal). Over the weeks, by specifically targeting off-task and on-task behaviours, the teacher taught Andrew a wide, positive behaviour repertoire.

This book is about behaviour *recovery*. Its primary message is concerned with *teaching* behaviour to BD children in the context of colleague support. Teachers are used to teaching (even one-to-one remedial teaching) academic skills (literacy and numeracy); they tend not to think of specifically teaching behaviour in the same way. It has been my experience, along with my colleagues using behaviour recovery approaches, that a small percentage of children need one-to-one modelling and rehearsal to enable them to 'recover' the behaviours that those in the typical range have established already. If teachers are going to be successful (in any way) with BD children in mainstream schools they have to have whole-school and early intervention focus. Behaviour recovery recognises the demands on and limitations faced by primary school teachers and argues that schools (via the class teacher) can have a significant effect in helping students towards positive and responsible behaviour.

Note: References are made to the supplementary material available with this text. The supplementary material contains photocopy masters (PM) of key teaching plans relevant to the program. Teachers are encouraged to photocopy these masters when developing a behaviour recovery plan.

1

Understanding Behaviourally Disordered Children

*T*eachers are key caregivers in the lives of children. They provide significant emotional and social security, especially for BD students whose home life is often dysfunctional. But they provide this care at a cost.

I recall teaching with a colleague, many years ago, who had a BD child in her Year 1 class. Although he had an angelic face (in his better moments) with curly blonde hair, he often engaged his teacher in major power struggles over refusal to do work, pack up equipment or join others during mat-time. He was noisy in class and threw tantrums on a regular basis. Her 'support' included a homily from the principal on being 'firmer with him'. The principal noted that, 'I have no problem with him when he's in my office'. This banal observation underlines the obvious — that most students are OK on a one-to-one basis.

Teacher isolation

It wasn't until my colleague broke down in the staff meeting one day when discussing Craig's behaviour in the playground that any effective support was offered. 'Do you know what your Craig did in the playground!' When a student is disruptive in the playground, staff should take the approach that it is a whole-school issue, not just the class teacher's concern. *All* teachers have a 'duty-of-care' role for *all* students when outside the classroom. The problem in this school was the tacit acceptance of structural isolation. 'He's really your problem.' While the staff didn't say this in so many words there had never been any constructive problem solving with all the parties, or any offers of pupil-sharing (rotating him in other classes to give the teacher a break) or constructive use of time-out or remediation for the student concerned. This tacit acceptance of structural isolation ('It's your class, your problem') is damaging to teacher welfare. Even if the teacher is utilising ineffective management practices, merely lecturing or blaming is only going to make matters worse.

Part of the problem is teachers' natural reluctance to share concerns or problems (with senior staff especially) for fear they may be seen as failures. As difficult is the reality that senior staff, or colleagues, may feel that if they offer support it may be seen as implying weakness — as a result no one is really helped. Teaching tends to perpetuate structural isolation — but this is changing. More and more teachers are realising that the only effective way to develop positive behaviour management across a school is in the context of a supportive school environment where colleague support is the norm.

A supportive ethos

All teachers need to know that whenever a student's behaviour profile is significantly disturbing (see p. 17) that the information is shared and due processes set in place. This due process is based around colleague support and an acknowledgement that this support is *normative*, not a special favour to any one teacher. The throw-away lines, 'I'm glad I don't have that little ____ in my room' or 'If he was in my room I'd show the little ____ who's in control!' are not much help either. It is essential the class teacher feels she does not have to cope alone.

Building a supportive culture in a school is not easy — it takes time and will need to be endorsed and modelled by senior administration. It involves emotional, structural and problem-solving support. It may also include elective classroom observations and non-judgemental feedback as a way of gaining insight into classroom behaviour and as a vehicle for professional development (Rogers 1992a). Colleague support for teachers with BD students involves all of the following.

1 A whole-school recognition that behaviour problems are best dealt with from a shared perspective.

2 Recognition that significant behaviour problems need a team approach.

3 Willingness by the class teacher to accept support and recognition that this support is normative.

4   Setting up (and participating in) rostered time release for colleagues who have BD students. (This time release will be used to cover the class while the teacher has recovery time with the student.)

5   Support of withdrawal of the BD student so that the class teacher can run a classroom meeting if so desired.

6   Moral support and recognition that a child's behaviour disorder is not the teacher's fault and any workable solutions offered on a colleague support basis. (This should be the emphasis on day one of the school year especially if the BD student's reputation precedes him!)

7   Provision of a forum in team meetings or staff meetings (as well as administrative meetings) to review the behaviour recovery plan. Support staff can give their feedback here especially if the plan involves playground behaviour.

8   Availability of peer support in classroom observations where teachers team up and cross classes to observe management styles and BD students in settings other than the home classroom.

9   Class rotation where the BD child is 'enrolled' in another class from time to time to give the class teacher a break from the daily 'wear and tear'. Even one class period a fortnight can help; a whole morning or afternoon is even better. It is explained to the parent/s that this process is to support the teacher and class and that their child will still be doing his normal set work. It is necessary to distinguish between classroom rotation and time-out in the parent's mind — this is not punishment. It is also important that the whole staff has decided how, and why, such a process is to be set up within the limited resources of the school.

Causal pathology

On entering school a young child already brings a host of experiences to a demanding social environment. His family shape, his emotional life, a wide range of learning experiences and values have already 'enabled' him to selectively interpret how best he can belong with others. Do his parents value reading, problem solving? What is the male role-model like in his life? How are authority and discipline exercised? What choices does the child have regarding his own behaviour? How is conflict managed at home? What sort of things does he get attention, praise, punishment for?

In any class of preps (first year at school) the variety of experiences can be staggering. Some, perhaps many, children have predisposing experiences that enable them to cope successfully with the demands of a teaching and learning environment like school — others clearly have not. Some come from homes where frequent shouting, yelling, put-downs, screaming and 'guilt trips' are the norm. One day nice, one day nasty — inconsistent discipline. Some children have to drag emotional baggage to school that carries the pain of emotional (even physical) deprivation or abuse. These children have no choice about these predisposing factors, about where they live and who they live with. They have little control. Clearly this causal pathology will affect their behaviour at school.

Other behaviourally disordered children have quite stable, functional homes but they too exhibit a high frequency (and intensity) of disruptive behaviour; behaviours frustrating to teachers and students alike.

To excuse or explain?

It is easy to fall into the 'blame' or 'home environment' explanation when dealing with BD students. I've heard countless teachers explain away children's behaviour. 'Well his home life is "the pits", his father is "an animal". What can you expect!'; 'His mother is on valium sandwiches — what hope has he got!' While all this may be true, the characteristic *attitude* may militate against productive remediation and support. I also hear teachers say, 'It's not fair, why should we spend all this extra time teaching him to behave! He should behave properly! They should teach him at home!' *Perhaps* they should. Perhaps in an ideal, fairer, more just world the child would behave well, appropriately. The fact is he does not — at the moment.

I've noticed, too, that teachers rarely say, 'Oh, we won't do any remedial literacy with the child because he goes home to a dump where they never read, or take any interest in reading so why bother?' They teach (one-to-one if necessary) literacy *skills*, build children's self-esteem, work collaboratively to sort out the best program to assist them. They don't (at least intentionally) abandon them because they live in a dysfunctional home environment. Teachers need to apply the same mentality, attitude and approach to *teaching* behaviour. They need to be careful that explanations do not become excuses — excuses that the child is unable to change or the school is unable to do anything. I have noticed that teachers, or schools, who use the 'explain away' approach are the least effective in assisting these children. It is crucial that outside factors are not taken up and used as *excuses* — as if there's nothing that can be done at school.

A child spends a third of his day at school. During that time teachers can provide programs, options, a disciplined framework that can teach him alternatives to give a purposeful sense of belonging and increase behavioural

control. Crucial to this aim is the approach by teachers that emphasises behavioural choice. If a child comes to school predisposed to making poor, 'bad' or wrong choices, behaviour recovery can assist, teach and support him to make better choices while still reinforcing appropriate consequences when wrong behaviour is chosen. Rutter's research (1979) has shown that school environments (even in difficult socio-economic areas) can affect behaviour for the good.

Disruptive behaviour or behaviour disorder?

Many children exhibit 'naughty', inappropriate, irresponsible, wrong, rule-breaking behaviours (I did!). BD behaviour is different. 'What often makes these behaviours deviant, and the children in them in conflict, is the fact that the behaviours are exhibited in the wrong places, at the wrong time, in the presence of the wrong people and to an inappropriate degree.' (Apter in Morgan & Jenson 1988).

Teachers rightly get annoyed (even angry) and complain about disruptive behaviour such as:

- persistent calling out, talking out of turn
- rolling around on the mat during instruction or story time
- motoric restlessness (hyperactive, seat-wandering and annoying others; constant rocking in seat)
- inappropriately loud voice
- too much time off-task, inattentive, concentration shifts easily (and quickly!)

These descriptions are heard daily in schools, the most frequent being 'noncompliant and defiant'. Indeed this aspect of behaviour is more frequently the cause of referral than any other problem behaviour (Kazdin in Morgan & Jenson 1988).

There are a number of terms (or descriptions) used for these children: conduct-disordered, attention-deficit disordered (ADD), socio-emotionally disturbed, hyperactive. While these terms can be used in a clinical sense, for the purposes of this text I have used the widely accepted term behaviourally disordered (BD) to emphasise handicap in terms of behaviour rather than (covert) emotional states. Schools have marginal impact, power or even influence over a child's home life. Teachers can, however, do a great deal within the school context. As Wragg (1989) has noted, disruptive behaviour is not entirely the child's fault, nor does a retraining, or corrective behaviour program, eliminate the need for other interventions (p. 8). It is essential that schools provide appropriate counselling, community welfare and ethnic aide liaison, alongside behaviour recovery. The key point to note is that while schools can directly assist, support and influence behavioural change they may have limited success modifying home environment.

Behaviour disorder is a term which describes deviation from the normalcy which can be expected from most children of the same age and under the same circumstances. Of course a definition may also depend on who is asked and when, and the beliefs, attitudes and experiences of the 'asked'. I have had teachers describe as 'deviant' what other teachers describe as 'annoying but normal'. Definition may also depend on the broad client group of students' socio-economic factors as well as the school ethos.

For the purposes of this text BD children are described in terms of:

- frequency
- intensity
- duration
- generality of their disruptive behaviour (Is their behaviour the same for specialist teachers as it is for class teachers?)

When a student's behavioural profile is significant in terms of the descriptions above, and has been considered so by others, including the class teacher, then behaviour recovery (one-to-one) is an appropriate approach.

Attention-deficit disorder

While parents, with the school, should pursue any causal pathology such as possible attention-deficit disorder, it is important to recognise that any remediation will have to involve working with the disordered behaviour. If Serfontein (1990) is correct, up to 20 per cent of male children have some form of attention-deficit disorder. The disorder is evidenced in behaviours such as constant fiddling, regular inattention, hyperactivity, high motor activity, restlessness, easily-distracted, clumsiness, inflexibility, low tolerance to frustration and acting-before-thinking.

Paediatricians and psychologists can readily assist parents (and teachers) with programs to assist such children, even with the inclusion of medication regimes. However, if the student is on some medication (as part of the treatment regime) schools still need to address the ADD behaviour through some planned remediation and support procedures. Behaviour recovery approaches give the child a framework within which he can learn new behaviour patterns to minimise the frequency and intensity of the disordered behaviour.

Teaching behaviour

When children come into school they have to learn to socialise, share, cooperate, attempt learning tasks (highly focused tasks) and cope with frustration. They have to follow teachers' cues and directions, follow rules and routines, utilise appropriate manners ('Please', 'Thanks', 'Can I borrow?', put things back where they found them, ask to go to the toilet etc.). Poor (and disruptive) behaviour is often associated with 'serious academic deficiencies. Academic survival skills [such as] attending to tasks, following directions, working on or responding to an assignment, staying in seat, and following classroom rules — are prerequisites to school achievement' (Morgan & Jenson 1988, p. 17).

Any behaviour recovery program will need to blend in with academic survival skills to build the child's self-esteem and sense of belonging. The student has to learn to wait, take turns, cooperate, consider others. School is a powerful social arena for children to negotiate. It is society *in toto*. Behaviourally disordered children tend to be poorly socialised with respect to their peers, they do not utilise the social and learning cues that most five to seven-year-olds pick up from the socialising and schooling context.

While it is easy for teachers to complain about BD children, it is more productive to develop approaches which will teach children:

- how to put up a hand without persistent calling out
- how to wait for a turn instead of butting in
- how to sit on the mat during instructional (or group) time
- how to stay in their seat for more than a few minutes
- how to speak more quietly
- how to move around the room without disturbing or annoying others
- how to (specifically) consider others
- what to do when angry

It is important to begin with a few behaviours at a time and not to overwhelm the child. It is also important to recognise that behavioural change takes time and success is defined as a decrease (over time) in frequency and 'intensity' of the targeted behaviours (see Running records p. 18).

Children have different learning rates and respond to a variety of teaching styles. Behaviour recovery uses the widest range of learning methods through pictorial cueing, modelling, targeted rehearsal, individual encouragement and feedback.

Lee: a case study

Lee, a kindergarten student, was not able to join in with the rest of his group for activities either in or out of the classroom. Although considered academically capable, his social skills were poor. In group situations he would sit on a chair on the periphery, kneel on the chair, then slowly slide under it head first. In physical education he would watch the other children but refuse to join in with the activities. Lee's teacher felt that if these social aspects were not addressed then more inappropriate behaviours might well begin to occur.

After discussing these concerns, and the appropriateness of a behaviour recovery contract for this situation, the teacher took Lee into another room while the rest of the class was at physical education. She asked Lee to bring in his felt tip pens and then she sat on the floor with a piece of paper. With no preamble she began to draw, knowing that this would catch Lee's attention (as he is a talented drawer). A representation of the class was drawn showing the teacher, the class on the mat and Lee himself in a chair. Because the representations were in stick figure form, the teacher thought that she may have had to lead Lee, but he was quite able to relate to the picture.

Firstly, Lee was asked who the larger figure was. He replied that it was her (the teacher) and, when asked how she looked, he was able to pick that she had a sad face. When asked who were the others sitting in a circle, he picked that they were the other children and that they too looked sad. He was also able to identify himself as the person sitting on the chair. (Here the teacher wrote Lee's name under this figure.)

She then asked why did he think everyone was sad and he replied it was because he was not sitting in the circle. The teacher agreed that everyone was sad because not everyone was sitting in the circle. She then drew a diagonal line through this picture and drew a representation of the class with everyone joining in, including Lee, and talked about how nice it was when everyone sat in the circle. She talked about some reasons for joining in (such as seeing and hearing things.)

(Note: This feedback is essential as it includes the social reasons for appropriate behaviours).

Following this talk she drew several boxes on the paper and explained that, if he sat on the mat with everyone else, he could put a tick in one of the boxes. She then asked him what he would like to do when all the boxes had ticks. He replied he would like to go outside and use the play equipment (along with the rest of the class). Lee was offered the chance to draw the pictures himself. However, he declined, preferring the teacher to do so instead.

With the rest of the class returning from PE Lee was directed on to the mat with, 'When we go back into the classroom and you sit in the circle, you can put a tick in the square. When the squares are all full, we will all go outside for a special group activity'. What was helpful, here, was the emphasis on group rewards rather than individual rewards. (This increases the child's peer support.) Lee immediately went and joined the rest of the class who were forming a circle on the mat. Several children (and a student teacher) recognised that Lee was sitting in the circle, obviously aware that this was something that he did not usually do. The next time that a circle was formed, Lee again joined in and so earned another tick.

It might be worthwhile to note here that Lee chose to keep the contract 'private'. It stayed in the teacher's office and he could go in to mark the squares off. The first time this occurred he wandered off to the office. After a few minutes, noting he had not returned, the teacher went to find him. She found him in the office looking forlorn. When asked what was wrong, he simply said 'I don't know how to do a tick'. (The things we take for granted!)

The following day Lee joined in with the next two class circles (his peers on the mat) and so filled the squares. The teacher talked to the class, 'I am really pleased that Lee has been joining in our circles. Because of this we will all go outside to play on the equipment'.

The following week Lee was on one more contract (several ticks) and joined in the circles with no problems. It seemed that he had learned the appropriate way to behave and was gaining the social approval of his peers. They mentioned the fact that he was joining in during the second contract and then accepted it as the norm. A gauge of the success of the program is seen in the following incident. From the start of the year, as well as refusing or being unable to join in the class circles, Lee had withdrawn into himself and become quite defensive whenever he had been spoken to about his behaviour. Shortly after going off the contracts he was involved in an incident with a Downs Syndrome child who was being integrated into the class. It was ascertained that Lee was at fault and so he was asked to leave the group. The teacher was concerned about what this might do to his newly learned behaviour but felt that the situation required it. It was part of the classroom policy and was a logical consequence for what he had done. Shortly afterwards Lee was given the option to rejoin the circle which he did with no fuss whatsoever. Breaths were released, jaws dropped.

Since then (mid-term), Lee has been a constant member of the class circles.

Halina: primary school teacher

2

Exploring the Key Features

*T*he behaviour recovery program emphasises the whole-school nature of remediation and support for behaviourally disordered children. It is set in the context of positive discipline practices at both the classroom and 'duty-of-care' level (corridor, playground supervision). Its key feature is the *educational* focus towards behavioural change. This *teaching* of behaviour (one-to-one or in small groups) concentrates on modelling, cueing, rehearsal, running records, feedback and self-checking. The primary aim is to help the student be aware of his behaviour and 'own' it in a way that respects the rights of others. What is essential is that the process is educationally supportive, not punitive.

These are important features of the program.

1   Early intervention support for the student as this increases the likelihood of the learned behaviours being generalised.

2   Provision of a framework for structural and emotional support of the class teacher. This colleague support is essential to the program.

3   Protection of the due rights of all students to feel safe, to learn, to fair treatment. The charge (sometimes levelled) that teachers have special discipline for behaviourally disordered students is wrong. What is special is the one-to-one support *outside* the classroom to enable the student to behave more successfully back in the classroom. In the classroom he should receive the same discipline as everyone else (see Chapter 6).

4   Utilisation of peers through classroom meetings and buddy systems.

5   Emphasis on the whole-school nature of the program.

KEY PHASES AND ELEMENTS OF
THE RECOVERY PROGRAM

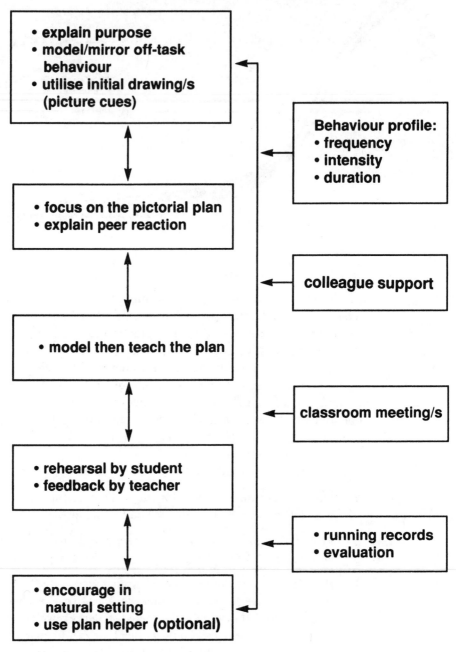

Figure 1

Establishing a behaviour profile

The earlier BD children are identified the less likely it is that they will fall behind their peers. This is true of any supportive educational–behavioural program. Using the *indicators* of frequency, intensity, duration and generality (of behaviour displayed) teachers should be able to utilise support for a behaviour recovery program.

In establishing a profile the teacher needs to be specific. Keeping a journal can help provide accurate information.

- How often?
- At what time?
- What does he *specifically* do?
- What are the reactions of his peers?
- Is his behaviour worse or better depending on who he sits with?

This provides a record of how many times the student calls out, butts in, wanders. How loud and disturbing he is. How long the behaviour continues. If he is directed back to his seat does he do so (if sulkily) or does he argue and procrastinate? The key areas to note are the child's:

- behaviour during the up-front, instructional phase of the lesson or at any time he is sitting together with the other students
- on-task activities at his table, or within a group-learning setting
- movement between tasks
- behaviour outside regular classroom setting
- movement and behaviour in corridors and playground
- behaviour on the mat during instructional time (calling out, rolling around, getting up and moving away)
- response to teacher direction during instructional time

There are many ways in which a profile can be formed:

- reflection on the teacher frustration–tolerance level at the end of the day
- comparing notes with specialist teachers
- keeping a daily journal (bad-day syndrome or characteristic?)
- using a pro forma checklist

It is important to keep some running records to clarify the teacher's own perceptions and to see (later) if the behaviour teaching program has had any effect on frequency, intensity and generality of disruptive behaviour. They can also be used to share any successes with parents and can enable a clearer picture of the student to emerge.

Running records

Keeping running records is not easy. Teachers have a hundred and one things buzzing through their heads day after day. Running records can give an accurate understanding of what is currently happening. Running records heighten teacher perception, give some accuracy to their reflection and can enable monitoring of any intervention strategies. The behaviour monitoring profile shown in Figure 2 is a *guide*. The actual recording of factors noted (frequency, intensity, context, time) is very difficult in the heat of the moment. However, it is feasible to use a simple notebook procedure and transfer idiosyncratic jottings or frequency marks on to the form ASAP. It's easy to forget. Having a pen and notebook handy for quick frequency noting is helpful (the *intensity* factor won't be easily forgotten!).

If the whole process can be viewed as a 'habit', it will get easier. The whole process will be less of a hassle if a comfortable procedure has been planned beforehand and becomes routine. These days teachers are used to keeping running records for literacy and numeracy. The use of this process for one or two students, although an added burden, helps in assessing intervention procedures, evaluation and referral (should that be necessary). Later the running records can be used to focus on how on-task the student is relative to the behaviour program. At that stage the focus of the running records is frequency of on-task behaviour over a set period of time rather than noting the frequency of off-task behaviour/s (see *Supplementary Material PM 7*).

Targeting the skills

The behaviour recovery teacher (preferably the student's class teacher) determines what behaviours need to be targeted. Essentially any behaviour/s that is *significantly* interfering with the safety, treatment and learning rights of other students should be addressed.

Before the recovery sessions begin, it is important to specify the skill behaviourally. These skills will be modelled, pictorially represented (on memory cue cards) and rehearsed towards reasonable success.

Targets and plans

A target goal for behaviour is the behavioural direction the teacher wants the child to go in. The plan is the framework within which the process takes place, and towards which energy, motivation, attention and encouragement are directed.

The plan needs to be a simple, achievable, workable one which addresses a few *specific* behaviours at a time. For example, 'Being kind to others' is non-specific. The child needs to be shown several particular ways in which he can be kind to others, then develop the recovery plan within those descriptions. With very young children even one behaviour is enough with which to start recovery. Target goals will not be static, however, and each new goal is set out within a plan (with its pictorial representation). Goals and targets can change over time as a child gains success.

The recovery process can also be adapted to work and assignment targets. Work is set out so that individual lessons are broken down to the sequenced and achievable — clear, simple goals for each activity until the child can cope with more generalised learning tasks. Memory cue cards can illustrate time on-task being broken down to three to five minute slots which the child can tick off or colour in. An egg-timer can give the child a visual time focus for time on-task. The teacher checks for understanding (by question and feedback) and opportunities are given (during recovery, one-to-one time) for practice of the academic skill. Of course this demands a lot from class teachers. This is why colleague support is the essential factor to ensure success of teaching positive behaviour.

Role of the class teacher

Behaviour recovery relies on a number of one-to-one opportunities with the BD child to teach him responsible behaviours. The ideal person to do this is the class teacher since she spends maximum time with the child. Furthermore, she can build in the encouragement necessary, for the 'take-up' (by the child) of the new behaviour.

For the program to have any success the class teacher needs time release for the recovery sessions. This time release is best given during normal class timetable time. A number of my colleagues have conducted behaviour recovery at recess times or even before school but some children naturally resent this, seeing the process as punitive rather than supportive. Ideally time should be allocated in the last twenty to thirty minutes of a given timetable period. If a child is withdrawn in the first twenty minutes, then goes back in to the classroom, unnecessary attention is drawn to the fact of his 'special learning'. The student should leave quietly with the class teacher once the support teacher has established the class. Alternatively, the class teacher can leave to go to the room she will use and, once the lesson is established, the support colleague can then send the BD student with a responsible student (quietly) to her.

If it is possible the first two sessions should be arranged within the first week (fifteen to twenty minutes with kindergarten age children). Most schools, however, can only manage once a week. The number of sessions needed is determined by the student's take-up rate. This varies from child to child. Remember, only a small number of children will be in such a program and all staff, will need to support colleagues who have BD students. A key feature of this support involves staff going on a support timetable (including senior staff — they will gain a great deal of good will if they do!) to take their colleagues' classes during behaviour recovery time.

It is essential that the class teacher maintains regular communication with any counsellor, ethnic liaison officer, social worker or psychologist in terms of the behaviour recovery program. 'At-risk' children often have a number of people involved in their complicated (and dysfunctional) lives; positive communication networking allows the best service delivery to the student and allows for essential support for the class teacher.

Setting up the process

While *any* disruptive child can benefit from behaviour recovery approaches it is normally reserved for those children who have shown resistance to normal classroom discipline and management in the establishment phase of the year.

A behaviour profile must be taken (see p. 17) and, with senior staff input, colleague support processes established for time release for the class teacher to conduct recovery sessions. It is important that *senior staff endorse and promote the policy that all staff support one another with BD children.*

The sessions

This is the purpose of the one-to-one sessions.

- Clarify the off-task behaviour to the student and explain why it is wrong. The child has to be able to 'see' that the behaviour is causing him to be unsuccessful in class; he may not know 'why' he behaves the way he does. (It is better to avoid 'why' questions.)
- Emphasise the effect this behaviour has on others (be specific).
- Model new behaviour/s (the plan).
- Help the child to rehearse them so he knows what the new behaviour is, and 'knows' he can do it.
- Encourage that behaviour in classroom time (or the appropriate venue for which that behaviour is being rehearsed).

After the child has shown interest in the plan most of the recovery time (in each session) is taken up with rehearsal. It is a labour-intensive approach but worth it.

With each set of behaviours the cycle is repeated towards a reasonable mastery (a significant drop in frequency and intensity of off-task behaviours and a corresponding take-up of on-task behaviours). Each plan is a framework for learning and mastering behaviour/s. The plan is drawn up in simple cartoon form to aid short-term memory. Some children respond very quickly,

Profile: Disruptive Behaviour

Name of Child: **Date:**

Off-task behaviour		AM				PM			
		B.M.P.		A.M.P.		A.L.		A.A.R.	
	F/I	F	I	F	I	F	I	F	I
1. eg: Calling out	U.F.T.								
	O.T.T.								
2. eg: Inappropriate loudness in class	U.F.T.								
	O.T.T.								
3. eg: Seat wandering	U.F.T.								
	O.T.T.								

CODE:

F	=	Frequency of disruptions
I	=	Intensity (on a scale of 1–5)
B./M.P.	=	Before morning play
A.M.P.	=	After morning play
A.L.	=	After lunch
A.A.R.	=	After afternoon recess
U.F.T.	=	Up-front time
O.T.T.	=	On-Task time

Figure 2

even dramatically, others take longer. For some there is regression before stability, for others the pattern is three steps forward, one step back.

The cycle of recovery for each plan normally follows this pattern (see also Fig. 1).

1   Working for ownership of behaviour. At the first session the teacher can model the off-task behaviour/s (mirroring), explain its effect on students (using picture cues) and invite the student to make a plan. If time permits the plan may be rehearsed.

2   At the second session the teacher goes over the plan again with the student using prepared picture cues, then models and encourages the child to copy (rehearse) the plan. The teacher explains how the plan will be used in the classroom.

3   Back in the classroom the teacher encourages, supports and disciplines the child within the rehearsed plan.

4   In subsequent sessions the child is given feedback and taught to evaluate his own 'performance' within the plan.

There are two extensions to the program using self-guiding speech and utilising the support of a 'plan helper' (a nominated peer, a fellow student) to assist in the take-up of the plan at the classroom level. This cycle is repeated with each behaviour plan as is necessary and with subsequent plans. The teacher will normally start with a plan for one or two behaviours and work to other plans as reasonable mastery is achieved.

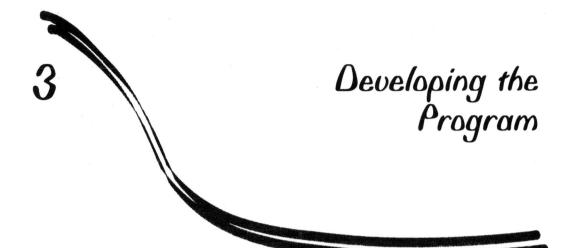

Developing the Program

*A*t the first session (of any behaviour plan) it is important to clarify why the teacher and the student are there. The tone needs to be supportive and relaxed, chairs facing each other with a table or two in the room. These will be useful, later, when modelling and rehearsal take place. It is also important in this session that the student understands that this time is not being used to lecture or punish him for wrong or bad behaviour but to explain why this behaviour is causing problems for him in class and that his help is needed to work on a plan to make things better. Rather than use long-winded explanations teachers can help students understand their disruptive behaviour by using mirroring and picture cues. In order for the student to begin to own his behaviour he first needs to understand it.

Mirroring

Children need to 'see' what you see in their behaviour. 'Mirroring' is an effective way to do this with the teacher modelling the off-task or disruptive behaviour to a student.

Ben: a case study

Ben was a residential student in a school for emotionally and behaviourally disturbed students. He was very loud when talking at his table and loud when calling out to the teacher. I began the first session by explaining that he was very loud in class and that this was concerning the other students because . . . Then I quietly asked if I could show him what I meant. 'Yeah, if yer like!' He grinned, responding to what I'd hoped was my positive body language. 'Look, you be your mate, Brian, I'll sit next to you here, OK? Now let me give you a demo.' I asked very loudly for one of the pencils I'd put on the table (Ben was often inappropriately loud in conversational talk). I then modelled how he called out to get teacher attention by clicking my fingers. I winked, 'Is that right Ben?' He grinned (boys often do). 'That's what I see you doing, Ben.' Here I'd returned to my normal voice. We then went on to make a plan to talk in a quieter voice in class, and get the teacher's attention appropriately. I did this by showing him a picture of him speaking in an inappropriately loud voice and calling out with his hand up. A second picture was added showing him speaking in a quieter voice (conversationally) and putting his hand up without calling out. I then modelled the new (target) behaviour which became his plan.

The purpose of mirroring is to briefly model the behaviour so the student sees it as clearly possible in a controlled setting. It's like holding up a mirror so he can see himself. 'This is what I see you doing — let me show you.'

I worked with Justin in Year 1 who repeatedly rolled under the table making guttural noises during instructional and group (on the mat) time. During the ownership session I rolled under the table and mimicked the noises then sat back in my chair. (Boys often think it's funny, even when they clearly recognise themselves.)

You must ask yourself how much of the student's behaviour you can authentically mirror. There should be no intention to make the child feel bad; mirroring is illustrative. Once demonstrated you need to refocus on the picture cues and emphasise how this special plan will help the child in class.

Picture cues

Mirroring can be an adjunct to picture cues that illustrate the off-task and on-task behaviours. A prepared drawing is shown to enhance the communication process. 'Justin, let me show you a picture.' The picture shows Justin under the table with other students frowning.

You first ask who that child is (pointing to the disruptive child depicted). Invariably they say 'Me' or 'That's me' and point to themselves. This is followed up with, 'What are you doing?' Then point to the children in the picture looking upset or annoyed and ask 'What are they thinking?' This question invites an understanding of peer disapproval. 'They don't feel very happy because he (me) is on the floor like that. They (pointing) don't like that.' When the picture cue shows the student doing the appropriate behaviour the student often says, 'They are happy (now) because . . .' In the second illustration peer approval is the focus.

I've checked BD picture cue contracts with non-BD children. With very little prompting they say, 'The others don't like it, they're trying to do their work'; 'The others think he's silly because . . .'; 'He should be sitting on the mat like the other children'; 'They are happy now because he's not doing that (the wrong behaviour), he's doing what he's supposed to be doing at school'; 'They feel happy now because he's not shouting and screaming any more, he's got his hand up.'

The mirroring and picture cues are there to establish in the child's mind what is happening now and that the behaviour is unacceptable and against class rules. The picture cues (in essence the plan) enable you and the student to focus together in a concrete way beyond the words alone. This picture plan will be the focus for that unacceptable behaviour during the recovery

Quiet talking

Hands up without calling out . . .

phase. Once this focus is established you can move on to the next important phase which is to 'invite' the student to make a plan with you.

'Let me show you a plan that can help you in class.' Here show the second picture cue illustrating the child behaving positively with his peers around him smiling. Supplementary questions in this phase can centre on:

- the rules ('What is our rule for . . . ?')
- why it is important to sit on the mat, put up hands, speak in a quiet voice, wait in turn
- the consequences ('What happens, or what will happen, if you keep calling out or butting in or getting out of your seat?' — be specific.)

- self-reflection ('Is what you're doing (be specific) in class helping you to keep the rules?')

Remember the first session will only be twenty to thirty minutes at the very most. It should be enough time to explain, clarify, mirror and show the student the plan. Finish the session by explaining that, 'We will practise the plan at our next meeting, OK?' It may be possible to rehearse some of the target behaviours in the very first session but if you sense this is 'pushing it' explain that in the next session the plan will be practised. Explain he will

get a copy of it as well. If possible, in the first phase of a target behaviour plan, organise a second session within that week; subsequent rehearsal sessions can be spread out as support is available. What the mirroring, the picture cue/s, the modelling and the rehearsal do is provide several anchor points, as it were, to the student's short-term memory. These anchor points are all positive ways to support the change process enabling the student to remember that he can do his plan.

Clarifying target behaviours

In the second session go straight to the plan as a focus for recalling what was discussed at the previous session. 'Ben, you remember at our last meeting what we discussed?' Get his feedback then show him the plan. Essentially the plan is a pictorial cue; a representation (in cartoon form) of the off-task and on-task behaviours. When I first began using these picture cards I called them 'catch-me' cards to emphasise, 'I'll be looking out to catch you doing the right thing'. The off-task behaviour has the child's peers showing disapproval and a 'stop' line going through the picture showing, 'This is what you need to stop'. The second picture shows the student doing the appropriate behaviour/s with peer approval.

In the example above Lisa is seen wandering during mat-time (she did this several times a session). During the recovery sessions I showed her the picture which mirrored what she did and then showed her the second picture with on-task behaviour (sitting cross-legged and listening). Before I had a chance to get into rehearsal mode she said, 'You mean like this!' and dropped on to the mat. She knew what was required and why. The next step was to motivate her to want to do that!

Cartoon pictures are employed to keep the learning process concrete and aid short-term memory. Students can keep a copy of the picture in a plastic folder on their desks, or in their lockers or on the teacher's table. The teacher will have her own copy as well. You don't have to be a great artist as the case study on p. 12 shows. You can use stick figures or the cartoon can even be drawn by the child. Some teachers have used photographs of students in off-task and on-task mode. Some have even enlisted the artistic services of a student from an upper year, to draw the plan on behalf of the recovery teacher. What is important is the concrete, picture cue card. Each 'new' piece of behaviour recovery uses one of these cards. Here is an example of behaviour targets used in behaviour recovery with a Year 5 boy (aged 10):

- moving around the room (moving to time on-task and staying in seat)
- settling to and completing set aspects of a task
- hands up without calling out (and waiting)
- keeping hands and feet to myself (no pushing)
- keeping all (my) materials on my desk

Each behavioural target card had its focus in a contract used over a period of time to 'recover' the above behaviours.

The double picture (off-task and on-task behaviour) is there to clarify, initially, the movement from 'old' to 'new' behaviour. This can be replaced with single picture cards identifying only the on-task behaviour.

Dean: a case study

I have included four of our contracts for Dean that reflect the target behaviours that needed modifying. Dean, although still experiencing many difficulties, has modified many of his inappropriate behaviours to the point where

he can participate effectively in the regular classroom setting. Eighteen months ago we wondered how we could possibly cope with him and support him.

Not only were the teacher and Dean excited about Dean's achievements, his parents were 'over the moon'. They replied next day that it was the first time they had heard such a positive report on their boy in his six years of schooling. Next term we are involving Dean in small group modelling situations where they [the students] will be taken through role plays that will identify positive and negative responses to situations and so further provide Dean and his peers with further choices re their response to given situations.

Jim: school principal

Rehearsal

The first step in a rehearsal session is a re-capping of the previous session where the mirroring and modelling of off-task behaviour took place. You need to model the target behaviour. 'OK, let me show you. I want you to '... (walk across the room quietly, use our manners rule, sit in your chair in work time, sit on the mat in class group time, etc.)'

When I first began developing contracts or plans with primary age children I made the mistake of just talking through the expected behaviours — and they promised the moon. 'Yes, Mr Rogers I'll be good for the whole time I will.' I wasn't specific enough on what the expected behaviours were, I didn't check whether the students understood them and I never rehearsed (practised) target behaviours. A basic, but significant, mistake. Rehearsal is essential with pre-adolescent children. It enables recall and boosts short-term memory. It is one of the most basic principles of skill development learning.

I can be kind and friendly to people

During rehearsal, it is important that the student:

- knows the behaviour skill, and its elements
- understands why it is necessary (motivation and need) for him to know and be able to do *this* behaviour
- practises the skill, gets feedback and support while practising it
- understands how the skill applies in the *natural* setting (take-up)
- receives encouragement and evaluation

- practises self-evaluation
- re-practises based on feedback
- is encouraged to 'hang in there' — reasonable take-up (even mastery!)
  will come

Wragg (1989), noting research by Jorgenson and Goldman (1977), points out that 'learning-disabled children both recalled less and *rehearsed less* (my emphasis) than normal children. When learning-disabled children could be induced to rehearse they recalled as well as normal children'.

For example, working with one older primary age child (Year 5), the class teacher focused on the skill of 'considering and cooperating with others'. This, however, was too global a goal so that student was then asked how and in what way he could show consideration. He came up with several elements he could *practise* in rehearsal and then apply back in the classroom with his peers including using 'Please', 'Thanks', and asking before borrowing (and

ELEMENTS OF BEHAVIOUR REHEARSAL

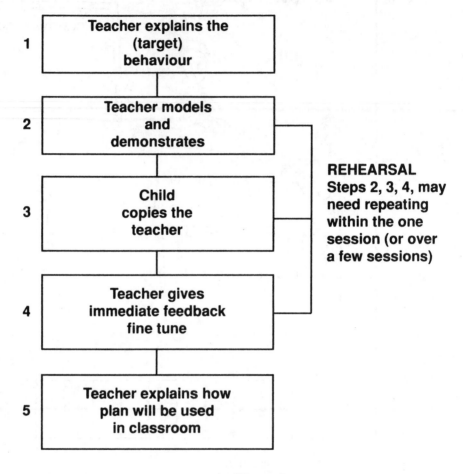

1 | Teacher explains the (target) behaviour

2 | Teacher models and demonstrates

3 | Child copies the teacher

4 | Teacher gives immediate feedback fine tune

5 | Teacher explains how plan will be used in classroom

REHEARSAL
Steps 2, 3, 4, may need repeating within the one session (or over a few sessions)

Figure 3

remembering to return) and considering personal space when moving around the room (saying 'excuse me').

Rehearsal has several elements (see Fig. 3). It needs to be explained how the card illustrating the on-task behaviour will help the student to work by the fair (classroom) rules and how it will help him get his work done, feel better with others, and make others feel happier too. Each of the benefits can also be rephrased as a question. 'How will this (point to the on-task behaviour card) help you to . . . ?'

I worked with a student, Andrew, who frequently spoke too loudly. Sitting next to him in the recovery session I modelled quiet talking in several ways. 'I bet you can (smile, wink) talk as quietly as that. OK, it's your go — you do it now.'

In effect the child copies your modelling. Talk him through it. 'That's it, that's the quiet level . . . good one Andrew. Now pretend I'm sitting here and you want to borrow my pen, you ask in a quiet talking voice . . . off you go . . .' During the rehearsal session give feedback to the child and fine-tune the elements of the plan. 'Do you understand what you have to do? OK, say it to me. Show me. Well done. You know your plan.'

One of the most common rehearsals my colleagues and I have done is helping the child to reduce motoric restlessness (seat wandering) and increasing on-task time. To enable the child to focus on a set time I use variable egg-timers (three to five minutes). In recovering sessions I give the child a simple activity (achievable) to do while at his desk or table and explain he is to stay in his seat until the sand has run down in the egg-timer. 'So sit here, four-on-the-floor (seat on the floor). What side of the desk do you want the timer? Where will you put the plan (picture contract)? Good. OK, I want you to do this (the activity is explained) until the sand runs down. Then, put your hand up (without calling out) and wait, I'll come and check your work, OK?' As he practises a three minute task move away as if you're not watching. If he forgets elements of the task go over it again a few times (most of rehearsal time is taken up with modelling, practice and feedback). With a highly restless child start with the caveat that *when* the sand has run down he can come to where you are in the room and wait quietly. You can then turn, check his work, take him back to his seat and re-start the egg-timer for him. With older children self-instruction (self-guiding speech), can be added during recovery sessions (see p 48).

Practice

One way of challenging a student's motivation is to pursue rehearsal through a discussion about 'practising makes what we do better'. (Practice doesn't really make anything perfect — just better and easier and normative.) People get better at something through practice. Ask the child what his favourite sport, game, activity is. How did he learn to do it? What was it like the first time? How did it get easier? Who showed him how to do it first?

Explain it's the same with this plan. 'This plan will help you to practise how to . . .'; 'My job is to help you practise to (speak more quietly, put up your hand without calling out, stay in your seat, etc.) so you can get better at doing that . . . so we can *all* work better in class.' That is, give the reason for the practice and explain why it's important for the student *and* the class.

Feedback

When giving feedback it is important to:

- focus on the *behaviour* (*not* personality)
- give *descriptive* feedback
- be expectant ('That's it Dave, I knew you could stay in your seat for that time.')
- avoid overload

Feedback can also be given by mirroring. 'This is what I saw you do. Let me show you again what I want.' Fade the prompting until the child can do the task without you fine-tuning.

Tony (Year 2) used to whine to get the teacher's attention and interrupt her with his work demanding she see it immediately. Over several recovery sessions she taught him to stand near her and wait (holding his work). She would then turn and say, 'Thanks for waiting Tony, let's have a look', give him some feedback and then direct him to go back to his table.

All this was specifically rehearsed. The second stage (after successful take-up in the room) was to teach him how to wait at the desk with his hand up (without calling out etc.) until she came. To increase motivation she acknowledged him with an OK sign and 'Thanks for waiting'.

Privately understood signals

Privately understood signals (P.U.S.) are helpful (and under-rated) primary reinforcers. Justin was taught to sit on the mat during instructional time (instead of rolling around). Whenever he did that he received an immediate 'thumbs up' sign and a wink. When Ben spoke quietly (according to the plan) in class time I would quietly say 'Ben', followed by the privately understood signal. Sometimes I would catch him looking at me and I'd return a wink and give him a 'thumbs up' sign.

During rehearsal phase the student can be introduced to these simple cues to remind him of elements of his plan. These quiet hand signals act as reminders to previously practised repertoire. Use these to minimise overuse of verbal directions and reminders:

- four fingers extended down like four chair legs on the floor (conveys the reminder four on the floor for seat leaners)
- finger to the lips and the forefinger and thumb closing together (conveys 'Keep the noise down thanks')
- beckoning finger
- OK sign with thumb and forefinger (encourages when the student remembers to do the right thing)
- 'good on you' sign, thumbs up and out (with a wink this adds a positive reinforcement)

I often ask the student (in rehearsal time), 'When I do this (the cue or signal) what do you think it means?' Invariably they get the meaning even before we practise it. I then point out that in class I will say (not yell!) his name and give him his 'special' reminder (P.U.S.).

In subsequent recovery sessions allow for feedback on class performance. 'How do you think you went in your plan, David?'; 'What part of the plan did you find easiest?'; 'What part was harder?'; 'What did you do that made it easier?'; 'How did you change from . . . to . . . ?'; 'What did you do to help *you* change?' If using a tick-reward approach go over the ticked boxes, show him that he has been successful with his (target) behaviour many times. Let him know where he has done well and those areas (specifically) where he needs to improve. Rehearse those elements again and add new behaviours as 'mastery' is demonstrated. The number of sessions depends largely on take-up back in the classroom. Some children may need several sessions to stabilise even a few behaviours such as hands up, sitting on the mat appropriately, getting teacher assistance appropriately.

The child should be asked if he wants a copy of the plan on his desk, in his locker or on the teacher's desk. Most children are happy to have the plan card on the desk as a reminder. Let him choose. Explain that during the day you will both look at the card to remember what he has to do in his

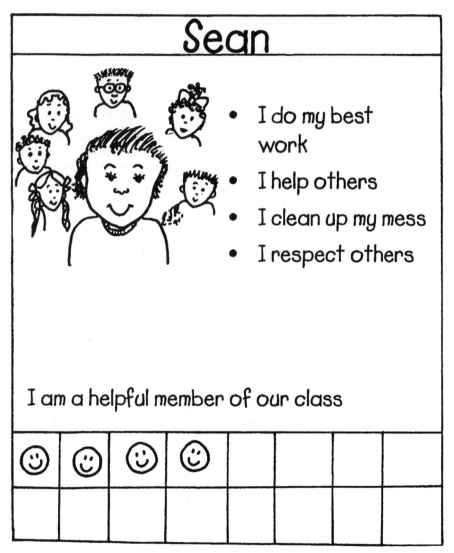

plan (you will do this especially when he forgets). Remind him (positively) at the start of each day, and possibly after lunch recess.

If using a reward schedule explain that when he remembers and follows his plan you will cue him and later he can tick a box on his plan to show he has remembered. At the end of each class period you can have a brief encouraging chat and look at the ticked boxes. As the contracts progress over time give the ticks (secondary reinforcers) with more discrimination (make them harder to 'earn'). The reward schedule can then be phased out as the behaviour generalises.

If some students complain about so-and-so having a special card you can make a general all-purpose contract card for them (I've done this) and give them stickers now and then for keeping to the fair rules and acting responsibly or you can raise the issue at a classroom meeting (see Chapter 5). Most students will be happy that the BD student is being helped to reduce his disruptive class behaviours.

You may need to discipline within the plan. Avoid 'why' questions. If he's not doing the plan ask him *what* he's doing, show him the card and ask him what he's supposed to be doing. Keep the discipline low-key but decisive (see Chapter 6). Make sure senior and specialist staff fully understand the process of individual contract plans and that specialist teachers, especially, get a copy of the plan and both encourage and discipline the student as the class teacher would. It is also important to receive regular descriptive feedback from specialist staff about how the student is responding to the plan in art, music, etc.

Emotional considerations

Teachers need to be careful how they mirror some off-task behaviours such as aggression with children who are being helped to modify hostile or aggressive behaviours. Preface by asking their permission. 'Do you mind if I show you what it looks like?' You could also use the same behaviour but talk about another child. 'Some children do this when they get angry. Let me show you.' Use the cartoon pictures to *illustrate* the hostile actions (touching other children's work during class time, using lots of swear words, kicking furniture, lying on the floor and yelling out).

The point of mirroring is not to embarrass but to illustrate. Explain you want to show them what it looks and sounds like. Then come out of the 'role', *as if* putting up a mirror and taking it down again.

Ethical considerations

There are two broad ethical considerations to consider:
- how 'voluntary' the student is
- one-to-one time

If a student is resistant and not prepared to cooperate, there is little point forcing recovery and rehearsal. Explain that you want them to help you with this plan. 'This plan is to help you in the classroom to . . .' If they still refuse simply let them know that you'll have another session next week (i.e. 'keep the door open') but explain to them that if they continue to behave in this way (here be specific) then, 'This is what will happen' (outline the immediate and deferred consequences). For those few children who use even supportive recovery time as a potential power struggle it will be pointless reinforcing that belief by threats or force.

One-to-one time has ethical considerations, especially when male teachers are working with female students. This should be discussed with senior colleagues. It may be advisable to have a female teacher in the room when a male teacher conducts recovery sessions. The female colleague need not be involved but spatially, abstractedly present (e.g. doing her work program). Use an area which is easily observed. Have a couple of tables and chairs to simulate class activities. Above all, help the child to be comfortable by being positive, explaining all the elements of the plan and helping him to feel 'in control'.

Student take-up

If Jason has had a long weekend with the 'dad' or de-facto he may bring the emotional detritus with him on Monday thereby making it a more stressful day for both Jason and his teacher. He may reject his plan (his contract) and regress on that day. I've had some teachers then say the program has failed. Not so. On the bad days you need to accept that it is 'bad-day syndrome'. We, too, have bad days, it's just that we are more successful in managing our bad days (generally). While never excusing hostile and aggressive behaviour teachers can be sensitive to the circumstances that may occasion it.

On those bad days when the BD child throws his plan on the floor, throws a tantrum, or acts regressively, accept that failure but still apply the classroom discipline procedures and treat him (respectfully) as if he's made a choice about his behaviour. Treat him as you would normally treat any student using immediate cool-off time and time-out procedures and follow-up consequences. He can go back on to the program later.

What you are looking for is approximation to the norm. For some children this takes longer. Like everyone, children learn at different rates subject to mood and circumstance. Continue the feedback and, when bad-day syndrome is recognised, teach him ways to enter the class on those days and deal with the bad feelings more productively. Work on identifying when he feels that way and help him develop a plan for managing it (see p. 95).

Locus of control

Behaviour recovery assists locus of control in the following ways.

1   The child manages his own behaviour in a way that *consciously* respects others' rights to feel safe, to learn, to be treated fairly.

2   The child's self-control skills increase so that he no longer relies on the teacher to always mark or check the work ASAP, come immediately when he calls, clicks fingers or shouts (and conversely sulks or whinges). He begins to wait in turn, stay in one place (sit during mat-time, stay in seat) for a reasonable time.

3   Perceptions and beliefs about who really controls (his) behaviour, relationships, application to academic tasks are strengthened.

4   There is an increase in social skills as the child relates more productively with his peers.

Increase the students' confidence and ability by practising the skills in a non-threatening way. Give feedback, after the student has approximated the rehearsed plan in the natural setting, refine, re-frame, encourage every effort.

Using self-talk

Cognitive psychologists have long studied the effect of self-talk or self-guiding speech on mood, emotional state and behaviour. The characteristic shape and usage of self-talk affects effort, tolerance to frustration, behavioural outcome and self-esteem (Meichenbaum 1977; Ellis & Bernard 1983; Bernard & Joyce 1984; Braiker 1989; Seligman 1991). The fundamental maxim behind cognitive-behavioural theories is that thinking, emotion and behaviour are inextricably involved with one another. Self-defeating behaviour is related to self-defeating thinking which in turn is related to feeling 'down'. *Demanding* assumptions and subsequent self-talk is often couched in imperatives such as 'Teacher *must* be fair'; 'Children *must* like me!'; 'Teachers *shouldn't* tell me what to do'; 'I *hate* maths!'.

'I *can't stand* it!' demanding imperatives are characterised by frequency, intensity and generality (they are applied widely and easily). A key feature of pessimistic or demanding self-talk is the lack of re-framing. There is no re-directing, just repeating the same 'explanation' ('No one cares'; 'I always . . .'). Realistic self-talk adds a qualification. 'OK, I failed, but I don't *always* fail. What can I do to make it better? What can I do to fix it up?'

Cognitive therapists have argued that significant and lasting change

includes a change in a person's characteristic thinking. Seligman (1991) has researched the effect of characteristic 'explanatory style' on emotion and functional (or dysfunctional) behaviour. Children can be taught that thinking is a special kind of behaviour. Some thinking makes them feel worse ('I'll *never* be able to do this!'; 'No one cares about me'; 'I *hate* maths, maths *is* dumb'). Other kinds of thinking will help them feel better (even when the going gets tough). If they can say 'This is hard but if I do my plan it is easier', they will feel better and *do* better. When children (or adults) focus too much on negative or self-defeating explanations they are less likely to feel like exerting the necessary effort.

I recall our four-year-old daughter talking aloud to herself in the car on a night trip. She was staring out at the darkness at the trees flashing past, the waning moon, the quiet night bushscape. In the rear vision mirror I could see (and just hear) her sub-vocalising, 'I'm saying to myself . . . I'm talking to myself. I'm saying the night might get me a bit nervous'.

Internal conversation is healthy and the more situation-specific the healthier it's likely to be. For example, characteristic use of global terms like 'Never!'; 'I'm just too stupid'; 'No one'; 'Everyone' ('Everyone is against me'); 'Can't'; 'Always' ('I *always* muck up'; 'I *always* get it wrong') are self-defeating in mood and behaviour. Children can be taught to re-direct their thinking (as part of their plan) because thinking is a special kind of behaviour which *can be taught*. As Downing (1986) said: 'By focusing on positive traits and capacities, adults can influence children to relinquish self-defeating behaviours'.

Teaching self-talk

In the one-to-one sessions you can explain (and model) the two kinds of thinking. For example, model a sulky entrance to class, and how the child sulkily flops in his seat, folds his arms and refuses to do the dumb work. While you model all this you say aloud, 'Hate this class'; 'Don't care'; 'Work's dumb'; 'Can't do it!'. You then ask the child what might happen if he says these kinds of things upstairs (here tap your head). You can show him a picture of a child thinking negatively or using self-defeating thinking. Again, the balance of teacher modelling, mirroring and picture cue helps to anchor the idea. So you mirror off-task behaviour and self-talk. You then explain (using a picture cue card) how angry thinking can equal angry behaviour. It is useful to generalise the issue. 'When we think like *this*, we feel like *this*, we behave like *this*.' Be specific with the behaviours, the thinking and the emotion (the feelings).

The next step is to re-frame the desired behaviour within the context of re-framed self-talk. Go through the whole behaviour sequence, saying aloud whichever self-guiding statement is appropriate.

Then model how the 'helping thought' can be said quietly 'upstairs', (here tap your head) and model hands-up behaviour. 'Do you know what I just said Sean?' If the child can't guess explain what just happened in your 'think bubble'. The picture cue card can contain the self-talk as a picture. For children who can read the self-talk can, of course, be written. Go over this several times as per normal rehearsal sessions.

Back in the classroom you can often reinforce the self-talk primarily during on-task time. Walk up to Joe who has been taught to speak quietly in class (rather than his normally loud voice). He has also been taught (through behaviour recovery) to stay in his seat for more than a few minutes. *When* he's speaking quietly pat him on the arm and say, 'Joe, I bet I know what you were saying in your head before'. Joe grins. 'You were saying I can speak quietly in class, right?' Even if he wasn't, the reinforcement acts as a reminder!

The degree to which the child can comprehend needs to be considered in terms of how much role play is presented regarding self-defeating thinking. Older children can comprehend ideas like 'When I think I can't I often don't even try'; 'When I think I don't care I often feel like it doesn't matter'; 'When I think hopeless, I act hopeless'; 'When I think angry, I . . .' With five to seven-year-olds leave the discussion about negative thought and go

straight on to teaching positive, self-guiding messages. Teaching strong-thinking, helpful thoughts enables the child to focus on this while rehearsing the alternative behaviour (find a tag that emphasises the thinking activity). The message needs to be simple and directional, often expressed as 'I can . . .' or with a when/then statement.

- I can move quickly to my desk, without disturbing others.
- I can sit on my seat without rocking.
- I can speak in a quiet voice.
- I can stay in my seat until the sand runs out on the egg-timer (or whatever timing plan has been developed with the student).
- When I get stuck with my work I can check my work plan again (check with my plan helper, put my hand up to get my teacher).

- When I make a mistake it's OK. I can work out a way to fix it (ask my plan helper or my teacher).

Self-talk can also be practised as affirmations, expressed as if the situation is actually happening.

- I come to the mat and sit with the others.
- I look at my teacher when she calls my name.
- I share with others.
- I say nice, helpful things to others.
- I walk around the room without disturbing others.
- I listen when others speak.
- When I get upset I . . .
- When I get annoyed I . . .
- When the work is hard I . . .

Within the reinforcement paradigm the teacher needs to:

- model the behaviour out aloud ('Sean, watch me. I'm putting my hand up and waiting. Like in our plan I'm saying, "I can put my hand up without calling out". You have a go OK?')
- ask the child to copy (rehearse)
- model the behaviour while sub-vocalising
- ask the child to copy while sub-vocalising
- check what was sub-vocalised and encourage the child to say this next time in class

Downing (1986) used taped affirmations which the child listened to several times at certain points during the day. These taped affirmations can be given by the teacher and the child, and listened to on headphones. Allied to the picture cue they become a powerful self-reinforcer that in time may become more characteristic of what the child will say in stressful situations.

The imaginary helper

With older students the teacher can introduce the student to an imaginary helper (see Wragg 1989, pp. 62–3). The child is talked through the behavioural tasks. 'You can . . . when . . .'; 'That's it . . . good you remembered. OK four-on-the-floor. That's it, it's easier to write when I'm not rocking in my chair.'; 'Yep, put my hand up to get the teacher over here without calling out.' The teacher explains that in class there will be a helper sitting with him, 'like I just showed you', all the time, to remind him of his plan. The child will laugh, thinking this is a joke. The teacher can even have an empty chair next to the child to simulate this.

T: 'You know who the helper is?'
S: 'No, who?'
T: '*You!* You can be your own helper.'

Here the teacher can explain how thinking helps (or hinders) behaviour. She can first model the self-talk strategy with the student then rehearse it.

It can be explained to older children that sometimes people forget (upstairs in our thinking) and say really unhelpful things. When they catch themselves saying these things they need to stop and remember their plan. Thought stopping can become a positive habit. 'I really stuffed that one up! I'm really stupid! Hang on, Bill (the thought stopper). It's OK to make mistakes; mistakes don't make me stupid. What can I do to fix things up?' Thought stoppers (Braiker 1989; Seligman 1991) put a check on the negative run of thinking so the thought can be recognised, and re-framed.

Again this can be put on to a small card with a catchy heading. 'Catch me thinking'; 'When I'm in control I say . . .'; 'Helpful thoughts equal helpful behaviour.' The students can have several helpful thoughts to remember when under pressure in the classroom. 'Take it easy mate'; 'Hang in there'; 'You can do it'; 'Count to ten'; 'Take four deep breaths' (Wragg 1989, pp. 53–6).

One student (Year 5) I worked with, had problems with attention and restlessness. He'd constantly turn around annoying others and was off-task frequently. The cue card had a picture of him head down with a talk/think bubble saying, 'Hang in there. You can do it'. We'd rehearsed that he had 'to go', head down, working away until I came over to touch him on the shoulder. I set my watch timer for two minutes and came over every two minutes when it 'beeped' to briefly encourage him. He did almost ten minutes of the language task set. The card sat on his desk, with the thought cue, alongside his work. He was being encouraged to be 'his own helper' with support from me. The time lapses increased from two to five to ten minutes (see *Supplementary Material* PM 17c).

Behaviour teaching cards: a case study

. . . (behaviour teaching) cards are a fabulous and innovative method for modifying behaviour. I have been able to use the cards quickly and successfully with a variety of behaviour problems. Teachers monitoring the cards have commented on the ease of implementing the card, and have also commended the card's illustrations which clearly show the target behaviour. The children's responses to the cards have been totally enthusiastic, particularly the pictorial presentation and the in-built reward/merit system.

I feel that these cards are particularly effective as they clearly show peer responses to the inappropriate and appropriate behaviour being exhibited

by the child. The card is also effective in reinforcing the desired behaviour. The cards may be used effectively in conjunction with learning difficulties programs to encourage children to read and write, and they complement on-task training with their visual representation of which behaviour is on-task.
Caroline: behaviour management teacher

4 *Motivating BD Students*

BD children often experience rejection by their peers and weary teachers who may not mean to reject them; they have simply become disillusioned at the student's apparent failure to respond to classroom management and learning programs. These students present as having poor incentive with limited effort. Frequently described as socially disruptive, the disruptive behaviour may itself (Dreikurs 1968, 1985) be the child's unfortunate (if annoying) attempt to find a social place — a compensating social place.

The importance of motivation

Motivation can be both internal and external in an effort to stimulate the student to positive action. Both will be needed, both overlap. Of course the ideal is (as is the goal of any behaviour enhancement program) to increase the student's locus of control so that he:

- consciously respects others' rights
- has skills of social interaction and on-task behaviour that don't rely on constant reminders or intervention by the teacher
- perceives that he really can control his behaviour and direct his rational world (Knight 1992)

Rehearsal time and in-class encouragement and feedback are directed to these motivational goals.

One of the important goals of behaviour recovery is to strengthen the student's belief in his ability to relate socially — in positive ways. These ways need to be taught.

The teaching cards depict social approval and social disapproval. These can be used to motivate the student towards social approval. If the class teacher (or tutor) has classroom meeting feedback (see Chapter 5) this too can be used to challenge the child towards the positive behaviours within each recovery plan. The classroom meeting feedback should only concentrate on what the students want him to do. Negative behaviours can be added as an 'instead of'. 'Your classmates want you to put your hand up instead of calling out.' 'Your classmates want you to (be specific) instead of (be specific).' It is also important to remind the class members to encourage positive behaviour and support one another's cooperative efforts (see classroom meetings Chapter 5).

During rehearsal (practice) and class time the teacher can use phrases like 'You can do it!'; 'Hang in there, you'll get it'; 'It might be hard (the work) but keep trying'. Encourager cards can help to develop frustration tolerance. These cards can sit on the desk or the encouraging words and pictures can be included in the picture contract. Plan helpers (see p. 59) are also a source of motivation.

It needs to be explained that failure in a task or failed effort at trying something does not make someone a failure. Repeated failure tends to lower expectation of behavioural or academic success. BD students need a significant amount of extrinsic motivation which is why many teachers have found the picture cue teaching cards useful as a directional focus for effort. The encouraging dialogue during the novelty of rehearsal, the immediate feedback in class time and the after-class feedback reverse the negative failure cycle. If students see they can achieve, they begin to believe they can achieve again. Success breeds success.

If the student uses an inordinate amount of negative self-talk ('I never get it right'; 'I'm always in trouble'; 'No one likes me or plays with me'; 'Everyone is against me'; 'It won't make any difference') it needs to be countered with the positive talk-aloud statements (see pp. 49–50). The talk-aloud statements can be rehearsed as part of the plan to increase internal motivation.

Motivation and self-esteem are powerfully linked. As the teacher and his peers begin to value the child, behavioural success enhances his value (esteem) of himself. Extrinsic esteem increases self-esteem. If the student participates in self-esteem programs that are part of the classroom curriculum for all students there will be significant overlap with the messages he is receiving in recovery time. Class teachers (in most cases) are 'significant others' in the lives of students. The special one-to-one time that behaviour recovery allows is itself a powerful extrinsic motivator.

Each plan that forms part of the recovery process can be linked to extrinsic rewards. At the bottom of each card are 'boxes' that can be ticked off, or shaded in, several times a day on direction from the teacher. Each ticked or shaded box signifies an occasion when the student has kept to his plan. Many teachers use these extrinsic motivators to 'kick-start' the success needed for BD students. When all the boxes are ticked or shaded the student can trade in his effort for a 'reward' (free-time activity, stamps/stickers, voucher at the canteen or even a whole-class reward. As each card is filled in (for each set of behaviours) the prompting should fade, the number of boxes increased — or shaded in after several (rather than each) occurrence of the on-task behaviour.

When planning 'academic' work for BD students it is important to discuss with the special needs teacher how best to pitch the work for likely success. The way the work is set out and scheduled is important. Workplans, with the set tasks broken down into achievable timeslots, help keep the focus in view.

The most important motivator is the teacher and her belief in the child. Of course these children weary teachers, of course they get frustrated (even exasperated at times) — that's natural. However, if they repair and re-build each day, the message, 'I believe you can do it', is likely to get through.

Teacher expectations

Teacher attitude and expectations are constantly conveyed and picked up by students in the following ways.

- The *kind* of attention given. (It is easier to attend to 'brighter', 'self-motivated' students.) Often teachers tend to call on the 'brighter' students to the exclusion of others (especially BD students). This is exacerbated *because* BD students often demand attention in disruptive ways (hence the need for a structured approach to develop positive behaviours).
- It is easier to accept mistakes or failure in 'brighter' children than to accept that the 'low IQ' or BD student actually made a mistake.
- The way in which tasks are set. (He'd *never* be able to do that.)
- Calling on students in class to contribute may mean, in fact, only expecting certain students to be able to contribute productively. This is where classroom meetings can be valuable in helping all children to believe their contribution is useful.

I once observed a teacher admonish a young student during quiet reading time because he had chosen an encyclopaedia to read. Worse, she did it publicly. In tone and gesture she effectively put him down in the very area in which she needed to build him up. Teacher expectations can be communicated through the labels they give to children's behaviour such as 'stupid', 'dumb', 'twit', 'dropkick' or the over generalisations such as 'You *always* . . .'; You *never* . . .'; 'Can't you . . . ?'; 'You *can't* . . .'; You should be able to do that by now ...' It is important to acknowledge basics such as using the child's first name, knowing his interests, speaking to him (acknowledging him) out of class (Rogers 1990).

As noted, most encouragement can be given briefly, even non-verbally. Wheldhall (1991) has noted that the use of 'contingent-touch' when praising (lower-primary) children for 'appropriate academic and/or social behaviour', saw an increase in on-task behaviour by over 15 per cent in some classroom trials (pp. 57–9). I have also noticed that the use of 'directional-touch' (Rogers 1993a) increased behavioural outcome and more positive teacher–student rapport.

For example, when reminding students to pack up, the teacher can come side-on to the lazier students and say, 'David, I want you to put the unifix blocks away now, then you can do your writing'. As she says this, she looks towards the blocks and points. She pats him on the arm a couple of times and leaves with a beckoning hand directing to the blocks. If he whines or argues ('But Angelo didn't put his blocks away!') the teacher will *re-direct*. 'I'll speak to Angelo, I want you to put the blocks away now thanks.' The teacher pats his arm and walks slowly away giving him 'take-up-time' (Rogers 1992a). If he refuses to pack up the teacher will clarify the consequence. When he does as required she can briefly acknowledge him, even with a directional OK sign across the room. If the teacher is spatially close she can pat him on the arm, 'Ta'.

This kind of encouragement doesn't take long. It is the teacher's conscious and characteristic awareness about her behaviour *in relationship* to the child that will make the difference.

Encouragement

Encouragement is basically enabling the child to develop his strengths; giving him courage to 'fail' and learn from failure, to 'grow'. It can be as basic as a wink, smile, touch on the arm, the 'good-on-you' sign (thumbs up or the OK signal) or the descriptive feedback the teacher gives about tasks, learning or behaviour. The key is what is focused on and how it is focused.

Damien: a case study

I was conducting a lesson on process writing (using the children's favourite authors as a framework for what makes a story exciting); several teachers had come to observe the lesson. During the on-task phase of the lesson I moved around the room, encouraging, giving feedback, a little corrective discipline here and there.

The most troublesome student was sitting by himself (as part of the class teacher's discipline plan) — the requirement was he work in isolation.

Walking over to Damien ('How's it going Damien?') I noticed he had written a great deal. 'Messily' — yes, and with 'poor' punctuation but positive effort had been applied. I asked him if I could have a read. ('Yeah — course!') He had written a great little story, and was clearly enthused by what he had done. 'You've written heaps, and you're still not finished Damien. Well done, hang in there.' I thought I'd call his teacher over to have a look (she was sitting at the back of the room observing). She came over and I showed her Damien's effort. She looked at it (without asking before she picked it up) and said, 'Yes, Mr Rogers, but did you notice how messy the writing is?' It wasn't just her pursed lips, her controlled 'Snappy-Tom' voice, it was the focus; she totally missed the effort.

Some teachers believe that if they *don't* criticise nothing will change or get done. The purpose of encouragement lies not in false praise ('Good boy', 'Good girl') but in focusing, and helping the student to focus, on the effort given or required for a task. It is important to use descriptive feedback rather than *mere* criticism. Children need to know where they are going wrong (or not achieving a target). This is best done quietly, without unnecessary embarrassment and in some cases is most effective on a one-to-one basis. BD students can be taught to self-correct daily and in recovery (one-to-one) sessions using questions such as these.

- What was the easiest part of your plan today (or this week) and why?
- What was the hardest part and why?
- Can you remember what you did when . . . ? (Help them to recall both positive and negative behaviours. Mirroring can help here.)
- What can you do instead of . . . ? (Be specific about the incorrect or wrong behaviour/s.)
- What can you do *next* time?
- What do you feel when . . . (Be specific.)

Verbal encouragement

The hardest part about any encouragement is remembering to give it. One aspect of the encouragement used in rehearsal sessions with BD students is that it may spill over into normative encouragement by the teacher during in-class time.

- 'You did a good job of . . . ' (Be specific.)
- 'Thanks for working quietly (helpfully, politely, carefully).
- 'Great sharing there, Paul.'
- 'Thanks for waiting while I was busy with . . .'
- 'I liked the way you remembered to walk quietly to your desk.'
- 'Good manners there.'
- 'If you keep smiling like that (or helping like that), people will be

happy because ... Do you know what will happen if you keep ...?
(mention their positive behaviour) They'll be happy!'
- 'Good on you for ...?'
- 'You remembered your plan to ... (be specific). Well done.'

Another way to increase on-task behaviour is by telegraphing expectation. A colleague of mine had a BD student who improved through his plan by the teacher's use of peer encouragement and telegraphing expectation. She lined up several students who reminded the BD student as he approached their table or their equipment with phrases like 'Hi, Matthew, want to borrow a texta?' This gave Matthew a chance to ask appropriately. The teacher also backed this up with 'test runs' (similar to the rehearsed behaviours). 'Matthew, I want you to go to Paul and Lisa's table and ...' (Here she specified a positive social behaviour task.) The students would then give some brief positive encouragement to Matthew based on the classroom meeting suggestions on how to encourage one another (see p. 57).

As Rosenthal and Jacobsen (1967) have shown, shortcomings in academic performance and social behaviour are not merely explained by the fact that the child is a member of a disadvantaged group. 'There may well be another reason. It is that the child who does poorly in school because that is what is expected of him. In other words his shortcomings may originate not in his different ethnic, cultural and economic background but in his teacher's response to that background' (p. 184). Rosenthal and Jacobsen have also conducted a number of experiments that indicate all teachers know (in their more reflective moments) that expectation does affect outcomes. This expectation can be communicated via *characteristic* perception, stance, tone, gesture and inflection as well as words (Grinder 1991, 1993).

Rosenthal and Jacobsen randomly selected students who were allocated to teachers with descriptors such as 'spurters' and 'slow track'. The experimental treatment focused on labelling students as children who could be expected to perform well or poorly. The difference between the groups was 'entirely in the minds of the teachers'. What is intriguing is that the children, 'from whom intellectual growth was expected were described as having a better chance at being successful in later life and being happier, more curious and more interesting than the other children' (compare Silberman 1970).

I have noticed a similar phenomenon with behaviour and expectation. Rosenthal and Jacobsen explain that this expectation probably lies in the subtler features of the interaction of the teacher and her pupils. Her tone of voice, facial expressions, touch and posture 'may be the means by which — probably quite unwittingly — she communicates her expectations to the pupils. Such communication might help the child by changing his conception of himself, his anticipation of his own behaviour, his motivation or his cognitive skills' (p. 188). Teachers will admit, though, having to work against their feelings at times ('I *feel* he won't do well'; 'He *always* . . . '; 'He *never* . . . ') and remember to encourage when it is appropriate. Not an easy task but a necessary one.

Enlisting the support of a plan helper

One way to consolidate, and encourage, positive behaviour is by teaming the BD student up with one of his peers — giving him, in effect, a plan helper. The class teacher selects a few likely and willing candidates (those with common sense and positive social skills) and asks them if they would like to help their classmate with his plan. It could be a student from another class who comes in to do cross-age tutoring (within the plan) but it is normally someone in the BD student's own class who can sit near him each day. The job of plan helper can be rotated over several weeks if necessary. It is a surprise to some teachers just how responsible and supportive students can be in this role. The plan helper's job description is to help the BD child with his plan; not to do it for him (he can remind, encourage and help).

Part of Chris's behaviour recovery plan involved going to his class locker before each writing activity or maths task to get his egg-timer. He used the egg-timer (in three to five minute bursts) to focus on his task without seat-rocking, seat wandering, turning around. He sat the egg-timer on his desk, worked for three minutes, ticked a 'finished-a-bit-box', and then put his hand up. The teacher then came over for a brief bit of encouragement, or signalled across the room (see p. 41). With the assistance of a plan helper the teacher's role — to remind and encourage — was enhanced. The plan helper reminded Chris if he forgot to get his egg-timer, to sit four-on-the-floor, to put his hand up without calling out. He even used some of the privately understood signals.

Teachers can brief the plan helper with some helpful cue phrases for reminding and encouraging. When the BD child 'forgets', 'wanders', 'rocks', the plan helper can quietly act as teacher support. The other advantage in this support is the increase in peer-group interaction; especially when the BD child is encouraged by a peer for doing the right thing.

The role of plan helper is also beneficial in the development of social supportive skills and is at the heart of cooperative learning. The BD child will need to feel he wants the help of a classmate so he is offered three names from which to choose. 'Which of these three students would you like to help you with your plan?' The plan helper can even sit in on some of the recovery sessions (the one-to-one sessions) to get an idea of the target behaviours. It is explained to the BD child that 'x' is going to 'help you with your plan in class'. The BD child should be asked where he would like his plan helper to sit.

Peer encouragement

Van Houten (1980) outlines a number of studies that demonstrate that, while children frequently reinforce, or attend, to misbehaviour in their peers, they can also be taught to attend to positive behaviours. Key students were selected as 'peer therapists' or 'peer encouragers'. They were then taught how they could help reduce disruptive behaviour and increase the occurrence of more appropriate classroom behaviour.

After being trained to spot instances of on-task attention and desirable behaviour they were given instruction on how they could encourage and attend to those behaviours and what behaviours they could 'ignore'. They (the peer therapists) also kept daily records which they discussed with their teacher at the close of each day. The studies showed that peers could (by their conscious intervention) influence the behaviours of fellow disruptive students.

5 Utilising the Child's Peers

When a child comes into a socially demanding context like school a prime motivation for behaviour will be social belonging, whatever his 'emotional pathology'. The child, in effect, asks 'How do I belong here? How do I gain a place of significance, purpose, power? How do I fit in?' (Dreikurs 1968, 1985). While many children (fortunately for general sanity!) find constructive ways to belong, a small percentage seek counter-productive ways to gain social credibility. An understanding of this is crucial when relating to disruptive and disordered behaviour.

When a child repeatedly (and annoyingly) calls out, whines, wanders, butts in, won't sit on the mat during mat-time, won't line-up, join in, do his work, he is not merely trying to gain attention or provoke a power exchange. He is seeking to 'belong' *through* those behaviours. Within his own selective frame of reference he believes that these behaviours gain him a 'place' and, of course, when teachers and students, over-service (over-attend, 'buy-into') those behaviours the child's mistaken belief is confirmed.

The class giggles among themselves when Jason is under the table and his teacher is raising her voice to get him out, or drags him out kicking and screaming, or pleads with him to come out. The class giggling reinforces the child's belief. If the child refuses to do the work, or refuses to join in, or pack up and the teacher argues and verbally fights back and threatens (often with the work still not being done) the child believes he is powerful in this exchange. He 'belongs'. BD children are often alienated from their peers yet laughed at or over-serviced by them when they are acting disruptively. The long-term outcome of behaviour recovery is to enable the child to belong (and gain peer acceptance) using productive means.

Behaviour recovery utilises one-to-one attention in order to develop purposeful belonging by drawing attention to peer approval and peer disapproval. Utilising the child's desire to belong, the teacher can use rehearsal sessions to motivate that desire.

Classroom meetings

The personal satisfaction of a *positive* acceptance, of doing the right thing, of belonging in a worthwhile way is a central goal of all classroom management (and of behaviour recovery in particular). The teacher reinforces this by using classroom meetings to enlist whole-class support for the discipline plan. Further support can be garnered using peer helpers (see Chapter 4).

Most teachers use classroom discussion as a regular feature of classroom life; classroom meetings provide a more focused forum for such discussions. These meetings often follow a set time, topic or issue, and use open-ended or problem-solving processes as a framework for discussion. They are an ideal vehicle to assess student attitudes, concerns and opinions on school-wide topics such as making rules, playground behaviour, improving the quality of life at school. They can be used as a crucial step in forming school policies. If these meetings are a regular feature of classroom life they can be explained in the school's policy and referred to at parent information night. It can also be helpful to send a note home in the school, or class, newsletter when a particular meeting is planned.

Classroom meetings are a well-established feature of classroom life in many primary schools (Nelson 1981; Rogers 1990; Dempster & Raff 1992). Many primary schools use classroom meetings on a regular basis to allow students to open up a topic, explore a range of options, share opinions, think aloud, hear what others value, believe in, and feel about common concerns within a common forum. The meetings can be used to discuss an educational topic in a general or focused way. They can also be used to assess a topic, plan a program, evaluate classroom life. For example, at the end of each term it is worth asking the questions, 'What has worked well in this class (for you, for us all) this term and why?'; 'What hasn't worked well and why?'; 'What can we do to improve things, make them better?' If children are given genuine opportunity to share their ideas, test out opinions, share concerns and look for solutions — they are then valued. They can believe that they are given the dignity of involvement and participation in classroom life. They will come to believe that they and their concerns, ideas and opinions count.

If classroom meetings are used as a regular forum, an agenda board can list topics for discussion by individuals, or the teacher. In fact many concerns of individuals can be dealt with in this way, by asking the child, 'Do you want to raise this in meeting time? Do you want to have it noted on

the board?' This, of course, should be carried out only with the child's willing cooperation. Regular use of classroom meetings meets the social needs of belonging and participation, where self-concept can be strengthened, problem-solving skills enhanced, and a challenging and enjoyable forum for healthy discussion provided. In terms of supporting BD students the kind of classroom meeting discussed here is a problem-solving meeting. Such a meeting provides a number of opportunities.

- A forum for raising an issue of concern to both teacher and students (teasing, fighting, dobbing, bullying, swearing, noise level, put-downs).
- An outlet of concern for all students. They all hear the same things, the concerns, the opinions, how people feel, what suggestions are made, what the outcome will be.
- A forum for enlisting class support (with the teacher) for working with the BD student.
- An outcome agreed to by all the students.

Planning a meeting

Plan a specific time and topic. 'On Wednesday we'll be having a special classroom meeting to discuss ...' The topic could be in-class concerns, raised by the students or you, or it could focus on a BD child's behaviour in particular.

The seating should be arranged in a circle to enhance visual and auditory communication. If the desks are all facing the same way it is often difficult for everyone to hear. The circle plan allows everybody to see and hear everyone else. It is important for you to sit at the same level, whether on chairs or on the floor. Plan ahead how the chairs can be moved into a circle and the desks to the side. Brainstorm suggestions from the group and pick the best so there is a routine for all meetings.

Develop some rules for the meeting. While the rules for a classroom meeting are similar to normal classroom meetings, the focus of the relevant classroom rules will need to be made clear.

Communication: Listen and look when someone is sharing. Give others a go. Check with someone if you don't understand what they mean. Often it will be the teacher who facilitates clarification by feedback and active listening. In this you provide a model for the students. For the garrulous set a limit of five turns so that they do not dominate. Dempster and Raff (1992) suggest a novel approach. Each person has five counters or blocks, each one representing a contribution to the discussion. These are placed in the centre of the circle as each contribution is made. Once they've used up all their blocks, they're 'out'. A fair routine.

Treatment: This is the crucial rule. Talk about behaviour, don't attack people or their ideas. Don't put people down. (This aspect of the rule is crucial to enforce, especially when discussing BD students and their behaviour.) Use positive language.

Safety: Keep your hands and feet to yourself. Only bring yourself to the mat.

Decisions: Decide together. The group, and the individuals, have to accept the group's decision.

Classroom meetings are sometimes called magic circles (in Years Prep–3). Here is an example of the rules used in one school for magic circle time.

- Look and listen.
- Only bring yourself to the mat.
- What is said in the circle stays in the circle. (This is an ambitious rule.)
- Respect other people's ideas.

These rules were published on a large disc of coloured card and laminated. They remained in the room and were referred to as necessary. Listening skills were practised in small groups of three to six children to enhance the quality of listening in magic circle time. The basic skills were published on a large card with cartoons (laminated) and referred to by the teacher and the group when necessary: face the person; look at the person; listen with your ears; lean forward; keep still; active listening — repeat back what you heard; say what you think is meant and check to see if you're right.

Running a meeting

It is the tone set by you that largely determines how successful a meeting is. Dominating the meeting, disagreeing with suggestions or ideas or, worse, putting them down, work against the very purpose for which the meeting has been planned. It is important that you create and sustain a caring and open environment where students have a genuine opportunity to have their say, express themselves, make suggestions, and participate in decisions within fair guidelines. If teachers merely use classroom meeting times to dominate the agenda and force a predetermined decision, students will quickly realise this and merely acquiesce or submit.

If meetings are held on a regular basis it can be useful to build in a positive sharing time. Students are invited to share positive outcomes from the week, either general or directed to another student. Teachers often need to give several examples to start with (keeping a notebook helps because it is easy to forget the positive behaviours and outcomes of a busy week). This is 'compliment giving' (Nelson 1981; Dempster & Raff 1992). Specific positives or encouragers are important (not merely 'I like David'). 'I liked it when Jason . . .'; 'I was helped by . . . Thanks'; 'I noticed the way Paul and Maria helped out by . . . Thanks'; 'That was a great game, wasn't it. I appreciated the fair play of . . .'

Running a meeting is not easy. You have to keep the focus, facilitate, draw out the more hesitant, check for understanding by giving feedback and use active listening ('Do you mean?'; 'Are you saying?') You need to avoid judgement yet clarify what is being said. 'What would happen if we did, or said, that?'; 'How does that fit in with our classroom rules?'; 'Does that solution fit our test of a helpful solution?' (Is it fair? Does it relate to the problem or the behaviour itself? What will the person learn if the class does that? Does it show respect?)

Discipline in the meeting should follow the conventions of normal classroom discipline (see Chapter 6). Students can be reminded or directed towards the desired behaviour. Sometimes this can be done with a non-verbal signal. If a student persists in butting in, or seat hopping, or using put-downs, he can be warned to follow the rules for the meeting or sit out.

This needs to be enforced for the benefit of everyone. If the student will not sit out the supported exit provision can be used (see p. 85) and the student followed up later.

The range of topics for problem-solving meetings is as wide as the concerns registered by particular groups (teasing, noise level, bullying, particularly disturbing members of the group).

If a meeting is used to discuss a *particular* student's behaviour it is important to consider whether his self-esteem can take it. How hostile are the other class members? Will he over-react? Will the other class members clam up for fear of retribution? It is important, here, to discuss with colleagues the advisability of having him sit in or not. If he does sit in be sure to have him sitting next to you. If you decide not to have him in the meeting make sure he knows what the meeting is for and give him feedback later. During the meeting time he can work in a colleague's room (see p. 7) for the full timetable slot within which the meeting is held. One way around this concern is to explain (one-to-one) to the BD student what the purpose of the meeting is and ask him if he would like to be present.

Meeting times generally run from twenty to thirty minutes maximum (twenty minutes for lower primary age students), preferably the last twenty to thirty minutes of the timetable slot. Open the meeting by clarifying the special reason for it being held: 'I've called this special meeting because there is a problem in our class and we need to talk about it together so we can find helpful ways to fix it'. Go on to specifically describe the behaviour/s that are working against the fair rules. If the BD child is in the room he will connect, as will all the other children who behave this way from time to time. Some students may quickly 'cotton-on' and name the BD child. At this point quickly emphasise the respect/treatment rule. If there are any put-downs at all emphasise, 'We are here to solve the problem of students who are making it hard for others in our class to learn, to feel safe, to be treated with respect'. 'We are not here to make anyone feel bad or horrible. Let's use our problem-solving skills, OK?'

If they name a student in a non-threatening way simply follow up, 'What is it that (student's name) does that upsets, annoys, concerns you or makes it unsafe for others?' Encourage comment on behaviour (addressing the behaviour, not attacking the person). Enforce the no put-down rule decisively. Give the group time to discuss the kind of behaviours that the BD student does and why such behaviour concerns them. No judgement, just clarifying the behaviours, and giving the whole class opportunity to share how they feel about *this* kind of behaviour. Recognise that not all students will wish to contribute. If the BD student wants to have his say, let him. Some students are quick to defend their behaviour, others will sulk and remain quiet. There will be some natural whingeing, but just keep enforcing the treatment and fair communication rule — do not let it degenerate into a corporate put-down. Keep a record on a whiteboard as the meeting progresses.

After five minutes ask 'Why do you think some students (or the named student) behave like this (be specific)? OK, let's go around the group one at a time'.

Children are quite effective at playing amateur psychologist when it comes to *other people's* behaviour. 'He does that (roll on the floor, jump in the big dust bin, push in line) because he wants us all to laugh at him'; 'He thinks that's smart!'; 'He's just showing off, he wants us to notice him all the time.' Children can identify the goals of disruptive behaviour well (attention-seeking, power-seeking, revenge, and withdrawal). Some can even recognise the active and passive aspects of each of these mistaken goals as categorised by Dreikurs (1968, 1985).

It's worth discussing as a caveat: 'All of us (from time to time) do annoying, or silly, things. We don't always behave well. We forget and sometimes we, too, break the rules. The difference with some children (consider here whether you will name the BD student) is that they (or he) do these things (refer to the list on the whiteboard) lots of times and are often not following our classroom rules'. Supplementary questions can help here. 'When students roll on the floor, snatch your work, spit, shove, what do we do? If we laugh or hit back what happens?' Allow some discussion on the way our behaviour can affect his (or theirs).

The last point to discuss concerns finding solutions. 'What do you think we (as a class) can do to help him (or students who do behave like this) to remember our rules?' Use terms familiar to that age group. The common response from children is 'We can ignore him when he does silly (attention-seeking) things like . . .' If they suggest ignoring as a strategy explain what ignoring means. Explain the difference between *tactical* ignoring and blind ignorance. Ask them what behaviours can be appropriately ignored and what behaviours cannot be ignored (safety infringements, significant teasing, physical aggression, damaging or abusing personal property, bullying).

Here are the sort of responses children commonly offer.

- 'We can help him to do the right thing'; 'We can help him if he's trying.' Ask for specific suggestions.
- 'We can stop teasing him, and picking on him. (Some students actively tease BD students.)
- 'We can tell him what we don't like, and tell him to stop it.' Briefly remind them of helpful ways to say their piece when being hassled by others.
- 'We can remind him of our class rule.'
- 'One of us can sit with him and work with him and help him.' (The plan helper idea.)

Students will often raise the need for teacher help and time-out if the BD student does not change. Assure the group that no student has the right to be abusive, bullying, aggressive, or keep interrupting others learning. Remind them (and the BD student/s listening will hear their peers discuss this). If consequences, or an action plan, for this behaviour is suggested be sure to focus on the 3 R's (Nelson 1981).

1   Is the solution (or proposed consequence) *related* to the problem? 'If we do that what will he learn?' Some students propose draconian legislation for BD students and will need to reflect on whether *this* solution is just revenge or whether it teach the BD student *about* his behaviour.

2   Is the solution/consequence *reasonable*? (Is it fair within the class rules?)

3   Does it show *respect* to the student concerned? If it doesn't don't use it. Ask the students how they would feel if *this* solution was suggested for their behaviour.

At all times keep the tone positive. Instead of condemning solutions/consequences use the 3 R's test in the form of open questions.

If the meeting is flagging, draw the threads together and summarise. 'It looks like the group is saying . . .'; 'It looks like we need to . . .'; 'OK, we'll close our meeting now, and we'll meet again next (nominate a time) to discuss this issue some more. Thank you all for sharing and discussing.' Remember, if your class is not used to classroom meetings the first few will be a little strained. Both you and the students need to get used to open discussion, the ebb and flow of open questions.

The value of having the BD student/s at the meeting lies in the fact that he is exposed to peer comment. A further meeting can be arranged where the BD student can be offered the opportunity to give a commitment about behaviour change. This is more acutely relevant for older students. This approach has been used successfully on school camps where a student has been hassling others in the dormitory. The class meeting proposes that he leaves the camp if he keeps doing 'x', 'y' or 'z'. The disruptive student then has the opportunity (after he and his peers outline their grievances) to make a commitment to change the behaviour. It will be important — if public commitments are part of classroom meetings — that the other students assist him in forming a change plan. It's one thing to stop certain behaviours, it's another thing to start new behaviours. A student may promise the world, 'I'll never do it again'. What you need to hear (and teach) is, 'OK, what can you do *instead*?' and then make a plan to do it. If a plan cannot be developed at the meeting the normal procedure is for the teacher to take the group's suggestion and initiate a one-to-one session with the BD student to formulate a behaviour change plan (see Chapter 3).

End the meeting on a positive note. Sum up the responses to the three major questions.

1   What is the problem?

2   Why do you (we) think we have this problem? or Why do you think student/s behave like this? (Be specific.)

3   What can *we* do to fix this problem and how can we help the student/s to change?

Clarify the proposals suggested and let the group know that you will meet in a week or two to see if there are any changes following 'our plan'.

Be sure to reflect on how you, as teacher, facilitated the meeting. Note the use of questions, reflective listening, management, time on any one question or issue, keeping the group focused and on-task. As well as self-reflection or keeping a journal, it can be useful to tape the meetings (it's only twenty minutes or so) or have a trusted colleague sit in. Remember, too, like any skill, conducting classroom meetings well is a matter of practice.

Classroom meetings *of all kinds* are a valuable feature of classroom learning. Children learn to describe, analyse and contribute to solving problems. They are especially valuable in giving students an opportunity to comment on their peers' behaviour/s, how it affects them, and to work on a supportive solution with their teacher.

In one school they explored the issue of problem solving in the playground and came up with the following strategies. Each suggestion had a cartoon accompanying it.

- Stop and think; how can I solve this myself?
- Ignore the person (if I'm being teased) and walk away.
- Talk it over with the person. 'Can we please have our ball back?'
- Invite them to join in your game or activity.
- Try and stop the behaviour. 'I don't like it when . . . please stop.'
- Give them a warning. 'If you keep doing that I'll go and tell the teacher.' 'If the umpire says you're out, you're out. If you can't accept you're out, you can't play the game.'
- Tell a teacher.

In another school the issue of teasing was raised at a classroom meeting. 'What does it mean to tease? Why do people do it? What can we do when we're teased?' The solutions were similar to the above but one girl raised the old rhyme 'sticks and stones can break my bones but names will never hurt me'. While this rhyme does not carry the whole truth, as the young girl (Year 1) pointed out, she also argued that 'in my head I can be strong — I know I'm not what they say the name is!' And I say good on her. I hope she keeps that cognitive tool well into adulthood.

A classroom meeting: a case study

One day, when Matt was out of the room (engineered by me in conjunction with the principal as the little so-and-so was never absent — his mother couldn't stand to keep him at home), I called a class meeting.

I opened the meeting by simply stating what I'd noticed happening in the room. 'I've noticed that some of you are really fed up with the things Matt has been doing.' Then, after seeing nods and sighs, I asked 'What things annoy you the most?' The class and I had a really good clearing of the air. Then I told them some of the desired behaviours I like him to exhibit i.e. sitting on the mat, putting his hand up etc. I also asked the class to verbalise some of the things they'd like him to do (i.e. put the lids back on textas, be nice to them, say nice things).

Once I had them focused on these positives I asked them to recall any times when they had actually caught him being nice. I, of course, gave an example to start them off. It took a bit of prising out but they could relate some instances, when prompted.

Then I asked them what they were doing or saying to Matt when he was being nice. We discussed feelings, particularly anger, and I began to draw parallels between Matt's behaviour and their own so that they could see how similar he was to them in a lot of ways.

I decided to use the analogy of a key and described the heart as having a door but in Matt's case it was often locked. I told them that they open the door to their hearts all the time and wonderful things come out. I focused on a few individuals who have model behaviour and reinforced their good natures. 'I can't see the door to Rebecca's heart but I know it's open because she is smiling.' I then looked at Rebecca and said 'But your door isn't always open like that. When someone says something horrible to you I feel your door close up tight. It's a very unusual door you have in your heart. It works two ways and sometimes the other side opens and the bad comes out and you say something horrible and hurtful. Has anyone ever felt that happen to their door? Why does it happen?'

After discussing cause and effect with them I said, 'Everyone has a key to the door in your heart. The same key fits everybody's door. If you say something nice to a person you unlock their good door and nice things come out. But if you turn the key the other way and say something mean, the other door opens and unhappy (and sometimes bad) things come out. You use your keys on each other really well because I feel the good doors opening all the time. But what about Matt? When his door is open which one is it?' Chorus: 'The bad one'. 'Well, you're the ones with the key to the door of his heart, you can open it. Which way have you been turning the key?' Chorus: 'The wrong way'.

From there it was merely a matter of discussing how to turn the key so the good door can open. They came up with heaps of suggestions. For the next six months or more I could solve Matt and peer conflict by saying 'Remember the key?' or by pointing to my chest and pretending to turn a key (a privately understood signal).

The best strategy they came up with was to ignore (tactically). They put this into action in an extreme way. I turned around once and saw Matt hitting another child on the head with a book (repeatedly); the child just sat there and took it, not reacting at all. Matt didn't get the attention he was after and gave up. I praised the victim for using his 'key'. After a while Matt was getting more attention for his good behaviour than his bad. It was also a good reminder to me to stay positive with him.

He now sits attentively on the mat, raises his hand, and is quite a popular member of the class. The 'key' operates without anyone having to think about it. His self-esteem is excellent. I can't change his home environment but he feels safe at school. The key concept is fairly abstract but a key itself is concrete. By having an imaginary key and a concrete cue children were reminded to stay positive and ignore what they'd didn't like.

Needless to say Matt will live in my memory forever.

Helen: primary school teacher

A classroom meeting and playground behaviour: a case study

Classroom meetings can be used for discussing a range of issues beyond the classroom as well. Here is an example of a classroom meeting approach called 'group' from a multi-age classroom (Years 3–6).

In the playground, as in any playground, some children were often mistreating others: fighting, name calling, teasing and generally not respecting each child's rights. As in every school playground, not all children displayed this behaviour. The children were invited to take part in something called group. During group children are required to sit in a circle at the same level (i.e. all on the floor or all on chairs) and to follow certain rules.

1   During group meetings children are free to comment on positive and negative things affecting their lives on and off the playground such as 'I like it when . . .' or 'I don't like it when . . .'

2   When commenting or raising an issue children are required to speak directly to the offending party/parties.

3   If a particular child has been taken to task over an offending behaviour that child then has the right to reply.

4   An appointed child named as Facilitator directs each session. This position is rotated so that each child experiences the role.

5   *When someone is speaking everyone else listens and awaits their turn to speak. This comes under the jurisdiction of the Facilitator.*

6   *Once a problem/issue has been openly discussed by both parties and the offending behaviour identified, the Facilitator invites other children to respond. Solutions for and/or consequences of a repeat of that same behaviour are then suggested by group members. These are then discussed and voted on. The solution most favoured by the children is recorded in a group book so that a record is kept of all decisions made. These decisions are binding until the group decides to amend them. Children may refer to this book at any time.*

7   *Participants must be prepared to speak the truth at all times during these sessions.*

8   *The rights of each participant must be protected at all times.*

Initially, confident children were the first to raise issues with the group. As time wore on all children realised that each person was being listened to and playground bullies were being held accountable for what they were doing. Gradually other issues were raised, such as name calling or using other people's property without asking permission and so on. What really consolidated the authority of the group was that their solutions and recommended courses of action were binding in and out of the classroom. After five weeks of group, two or three times a week, the children realised that something more was needed.

The arbitrating system

Some children were still coming to teachers to solve their problems while others didn't dare for fear of retribution from others. One child raised this point (during group), and an extremely productive discussion began. At the completion of this session the children had effectively given birth to what is now known as the Arbitrating System. The system involves three stages of conflict resolution in and out of the classroom for all students, and the teacher, to follow.

Stage 1

Try to solve the conflict yourself. For example, if someone calls you a name you don't like ask them not to call you that name again. The second child then is not allowed to refer to you in that manner again. If they do you may move on to Stage 2.

Stage 2

Go to either of the Arbitrators (one boy, one girl; it is important to have a different pair each week so that everyone gets a turn) and explain what has happened. That Arbitrator then decides on the consequences of each party's actions and outlines consequences to any guilty party in proportion to their offence(s). Suggested consequences or courses of action are listed in the group book as decided on during group and the Arbitrators may refer to this book when they are unsure of what consequences to give. If the Arbitrator is uncertain as to how to proceed or if any of the parties feel that they have been treated unfairly they may move to Stage 3.

Stage 3

Any party not satisfied that they were given a fair hearing may approach the teacher. The teacher will then listen to each party and proceed as follows.

- If the Arbitrator is uncertain the teacher will listen and ask how they think they should proceed. The idea is to encourage them to take risks and back their own judgement. Teachers try to guide them into making a decision rather than take over.
- If one of the parties feels that the Arbitrator has not done his/her job in a fair manner they may approach the teacher. The teacher's job is to listen and, if an injustice has been done, justice will prevail.
- If a child is trying to 'put one over' the teacher he gets twice the original consequence.
- If the Arbitrator genuinely did his/her best but was not able to arbitrate fairly the teacher has the responsibility to speak one-to-one with that child so that he/she knows how to proceed under similar circumstances.
- If the Arbitrator deliberately neglected his/her responsibilities the teacher will work one-to-one to impart an understanding of why the arbitrators must do their job to the best of their abilities each time a child comes to them for assistance.

Arbitrators learn on the job and need constant back-up and support until they can function on their own. It is important that teachers do not take over but guide the arbitrators to make fair decisions.

Ciaran: teacher in multi-age classroom

6 *Disciplining BD Children*

*E*ffective discipline of BD children is not significantly different from the sort of positive disciplinary practices typical children respond to. As Kounin and Obradric (in Robertson 1989) noted, emotionally disturbed children in normal schools respond to techniques of good classroom management in the same way as non-disturbed children.

Discipline is effectively leading, guiding, teaching children to own (and be responsible for) their behaviour in the context of respecting others' rights (Rogers 1990). The elements of an effective and positive discipline plan involve a balance between prevention, correction, encouragement and support, repairing and rebuilding.

It is important for all students, especially at the establishment phase of the year, to be aware of the classroom rules for behaviour and the routines for the class. These include routines for activities such as how to enter and leave the classroom, move around the class, clean up materials, move on to the mat, pack-up, moderate working noise.

It is a good idea to publish the rules using class drawings or illustrations. Make the rules few in number, simple, enforceable (see Rogers 1990) and as positively stated as possible.

Consequences for rule breaking need to be outlined, especially the use of time-out provisions. Preventative measures also need to include appropriate (and considered) seating for BD students; task requirements need to be achievable, sequenced with appropriate materials and resources and include a balance of group and individual learning tasks. Individual task sheets for BD students can provide a positive framework within which success can be monitored and progress demonstrated (see *Supplementary Material* PM 17c).

Working noise

When establishing class rules it can be helpful to teach the hands-up signal and appropriate working noise by using the *noise meter game*. A large circle of cardboard with four coloured quadrants, white, green, amber and red is used. A rotating arrow (affixed with a split pin) can designate clearly which quadrant you are nominating.

The students are taught that *white* is for when you and students are discussing, or when you are teaching up-front, or for quiet reading time. White means hands up without calling out. Move the arrow to the quadrant and explain this; later simply use the pointer as a privately understood signal.

Green signifies quiet (or conversational) noise; you should be able to direct a child from the back of the room without significantly raising your

voice. Again use this as private signal after it has been explained a few times.

Amber, like the traffic lights, signifies that the class is getting too loud and the noise level needs to come down. Put the arrow on amber and wait until the students recognise it and the tribal tomtoms clarify the P.U.S. After the students are initially taught, the arrow on amber acts as a P.U.S. to strengthen student-initiated cooperation.

Red is used when the noise level is clearly too high and a brief verbal direction is required. Stop the class and re-direct.

The noise meter could be presented as a giraffe with the colours ascending in degree of noise up the neck (with collar!), a car going up a hill, a traffic light signal with four colours. For particularly noisy classes, points can be earned on a daily basis and the points traded in for a five minute conversation time (a couple of times a day) where students can sit anywhere they wish (as long as no one else is on their own) and converse for five minutes at the close of the morning or at the end of the day.

One way to enhance the use of the noise meter game is to appoint noise monitors in each group, or table, or area of the room. At younger primary age level the noise monitors can wear a badge. Their job is to remind their fellow students to respond to the signals, especially amber. Of course when students do respond cooperatively thank the whole class for their cooperation. Like most establishment activities the prompting can be faded over time. Teachers using the noise meter, with positive behaviour management, have reported they have significantly reduced the numbers of 'Shhh!' and 'Please be quiet' and 'It's too loud'.

Corrective discipline

Corrective discipline considers what is said, and done, to address disruptive behaviour. Teachers need to consider how to correct:

- without being long-winded
- without over-servicing attention-seeking or power-seeking by the child (especially in front of the child's peers)
- without using sarcasm, embarrassment, intentional public shaming or persistent criticism
- by addressing the problem behaviour (and not attacking the person)

This is a tall order. These protocols, though, are essential in maintaining a positive corrective climate for *all* students, not just BD students. Even when you are angry with students, or when you have to use unambiguous command language (such as in safety settings) you can be clear about your anger without intentionally belittling the child. There are a number of strategies which can be adopted which help develop this positive climate.

It is useful to give commands with a brief, sharp, attention-getting tone (lift the voice) then drop to a firm, assertive voice and posture to give the actual command. For example, 'Michael (raise the voice then pause), move over there now' (said in a normal voice). The command can be *repeated* if he still doesn't move. A few words said again are better than many words said in a high-pitched angry voice. That unsettles the audience as well as the target student.

When faced with disruptive behaviour, you need to calm yourself first and then the child. Count to three and remember what you had decided you'd do 'on-the-spot'. You'll get better at this if your discipline is planned — ahead of time. It's very hard to calm a recalcitrant child if you are speaking loudly, or shouting, or threatening or grabbing and shaking the child ('Wake up to yourself and do what I say!'). While it is appropriate to *raise* the voice at times it is important to then drop the voice (when attention is gained) and speak in a firm, clear, slower, decisive voice. If you *keep* the voice at the same level of sharpness and loudness you are very likely to exacerbate further hostility (or aggression) in the disruptive child, and create unnecessary anxiety in the children observing the fracas!

Positive correction considers what is said, and how it is said, in discipline transactions both in content and 'tone'. As Grinder (1993) notes: '80 per cent of a teacher's communication is non-verbal'. Sarcasm, hostility, impatience, threat, aggression can all be conveyed in language tone with proximity and bodily gesture (such as pointing at a student). Coming side-on to a student during on-task correction is less threatening (in tone and gesture) than coming face-on and pointing (Rogers 1991b, 1993a).

Language of discipline

Planning the language of discipline is very important. Avoid overuse of 'no' and 'don't'. If a student wishes to, for example, go to the toilet during instructional time avoid 'No, you can't'. Use *conditional directions*: yes/when, after/then, when/then. ('*After* we've had morning talk *then* you can go to the toilet.') Conditionals are heard more positively than negative directions ('No, you can't go now because . . . ').

Use direct questions rather than indirect when correcting. Avoid the use of 'why'. ('Why are you out of your seat?'; 'Why are you calling out?'; 'Why haven't you started work?'; 'Why do you want to go to the toilet now, why didn't you go at recess?')

Two students are being silly with their rulers (sword-fighting). The teacher calls over one of them and asks 'George, what are you doing?' (Her voice is firm not nasty, her eye-contact stable.) The child says, 'Nothing!' (in a sulky voice). The teacher gives brief feedback: 'I saw you hitting Timmy with your ruler'. 'But we were only muckin' 'round', whines George. The teacher replies with a secondary question. 'What are you supposed to be doing?' (This directs and focuses the student's attention on the present on-task issue; not secondary issues. He is required to suggest the appropriate behaviour (or solution), with the teacher's help, if necessary.) 'Our work', sighs George. 'OK, off you go, I'll come and check in a moment.' She touches George with a positive, directional touch on the arm as he goes back to his seat. A little later she notices him actually working at his table. She gently calls across to George, he looks annoyed. 'What?' The teacher gives him an OK sign with her hand to encourage his on-task behaviour and George *sighs and* smiles back.

For this teacher the way she transacts in discipline situations is purposeful, not accidental. It is essential to *re-establish positive working relationships* ASAP. Any corrective discipline should be followed up by some re-establishing after the student has settled back to his task, or followed your directions or reminder. This re-establishing can be as basic as the example noted (a smile, the OK sign, or that word of encouragement). It will also include the practice of beginning again and starting each day afresh with BD students.

Use 'I' statements. 'I want you to . . . '; 'I expect you to . . .' State, or direct, to the behaviour you want to see: to the expected or rule-keeping behaviour, rather than behaviour you merely want to stop. 'Michael and Dean (pause to establish attention), facing this way and listening thanks.'; 'Pete, Kim (pause to establish attention), hands up without calling out — thanks.' 'Stop' messages need to be brief and quickly followed by a direction or direct question in a firm, positive tone. 'Stop that. What is the problem David, Paul?' Minimise loud replies from students by reminding them to speak in 'reasonable' voices. If they argue use re-directive dialogue.

Use rule reminders. 'Simon, we have a rule for settling problems, use it thanks.' Avoid getting drawn into disputes over property or friendship. If children refuse to take turns, remind them of the sharing rule or manners rule but avoid asking who started it or why they are arguing over the textas. 'We have a rule for . . . (remind them briefly without a lecture). Use it thanks.' The class will know (from the class rule) that arguing or fighting in class is not acceptable. The class rule will state: 'If you argue or fight you'll be reminded of the rule. If you do not stop you will have to work separately or have cool-off time'. Children need to learn they can't effectively deal with problems when they are really frustrated, anxious or angry. These are more effectively dealt with *after* cool-off time.

Avoid arguing or getting drawn into secondary behaviours (pouting faces, sighs or moans, last-word syndrome, excuses). Use re-direction instead.

T: What are you doing?

S: Nothing.

T: You're out of your seat — what are you supposed to be doing?

If the student is on a plan add the secondary question, 'What is your plan?'

S: (student procrastinates) But I wasn't the only one out of my seat.

T: (teacher re-directs) What are you supposed to be doing?

If the student hasn't started work remind him of the task. If he says he doesn't want to do the task avoid getting drawn, simply re-direct. 'Maybe you don't want to (acknowledge his feelings) but it's the work we're doing today. How can I help you?' Re-direction acknowledges or 'dignifies' briefly and then re-focuses the student on the central issue at hand (Rogers 1992a).

Establish a hierarchy for corrective intervention moving only to the most intrusive as situations or circumstance necessitate. This avoids the over-reaction some teachers make to low-level disruptive behaviour. Essentially a teacher can direct, re-direct, clarify the consequence, and apply the consequence. These four phases narrow the options for the student (see fig. 3). The widest range of options will occur with the kind of initial direction given (reminder, question, distraction, simple choice). For example, if a child is playing with a toy at his desk (or some *objet d'art*) a 'choice' is more effective (and appropriate) than a threat. Rather than march up, face-on, hand out, with the 'Right — give it to me! C'mon!', come side-on and give a directed choice. 'Bob, nice toy, I want you to put it in your bag or on my desk.' If he argues, re-direct, 'In or on . . .' As soon as he shows movement give him some 'take-up time' by moving away. It shows trust and enables face-saving. When he settles, come back and re-establish with an encouraging word about his work. Balance the language of discipline with the language of encouragement.

If a student refuses (in effect chooses) not to be re-directed avoid a power struggle by making the consequence clear. The student needs to know the consequences of continuing to behave thus. 'If you continue to do (be specific) then you will have to (the consequence).'

Consequences

All students need to know the general consequences for disruptive behaviour:

- work *away* (relocation in the room)
- cool-off time (in the room)
- losing recess time (the consequence at recess time can then be negotiated)
- exit from the room (if the behaviour is unsafe)

Negotiated consequences need to clarify specific future behaviour. This is the essence of behaviour recovery in that it specifies the off-task and on-task behaviour and avoids responses like 'I'll be good now' or 'I won't do it again'. Behaviour recovery emphasises the positive behavioural alternatives. It is important to make clear to the student/s (and the parent/s) that consequences are not mere punishments. Students choose their behaviour; positive discipline approaches help students make better choices. It is in this context that BD students are treated.

A consequence needs to be *as related as possible* and delivered by the teacher in a non-threatening way (her tone and body language is important). It is the certainty of the consequence that is more effective than the severity. A consequence needs to teach the student something about the appropriate behaviour (i.e. gain some *related connection* between behaviour and outcome). If a child damages equipment (or hurts someone) mere apology is pointless. The student can do a time/trade consequence — give his own time to do several positive tasks (civic duty). The responsibility of the consequence should lie with the child, not just the supervising teacher. Ask him what he did, and what he needs to do to fix things up. It is more likely the child will own the consequence this way. There are some children (very few) who resist almost all consequences (except time-out).

It is worth remembering that a student can't be *made* to do anything. The outcomes involve a balance of positive correction, cool-off time, consequence and re-establishing a working relationship with the student. Some consequences are, of course, best carried out after appropriate cool-off time; forcing consequences when the child is overly anxious, frustrated or angry may force the child into an unnecessary power struggle. Apart from essential use of exit and time-out provisions (which will need to be immediate) consequences can often be deferred until the heat has gone down.

Keeping running records

As with literacy and numeracy, behaviour development needs consistent reflection by the teacher through descriptive assessment. In short, checking if the program is supporting the process of behavioural change. This also provides basic documentation to administration, parent and support personnel (psychologists, social workers etc.), should formal inquiry processes be necessary.

A simple pro forma can be utilised covering:

- what behaviours are targeted for change
- what behaviours are disruptive (be specific)
- frequency and intensity
- what was done to address the disruptive behaviour (be specific)
- how quickly the student came back on-task

A simple journal or pro forma should be drawn up which is filled in two or three times a day (after each class session, if possible). A checklist against which a few words of explanation are made is a most efficient method. Even the picture card plan is itself a piece of descriptive feedback for the child, the teacher and the parent (see *Supplementary Material*).

Student evaluation questions

Teachers can use these questions to evaluate a BD child's progress.

- In what ways has the student's behaviour changed since introducing behaviour recovery? (Be specific.)
- Is there a noticeable reduction in frequency and intensity of disruptive behaviour?
- What have other teachers (especially specialist teachers) noticed?
- If you have a workable relationship with the child's caregivers what have they noticed since the introduction of the program?

- How has the student responded to the daily/weekly feedback and evaluation?
- Have any reward schedules been more effective than others?
- What are the most workable features of the program with respect to this student?
- What areas (specifically) can be improved?
- Has there been regular discussion with team colleagues while using the program?

Structural support

There are times when BD children get so frustrated by the demands of the classroom, act in an unsafe way, or behave in a way that really gets on the teacher's nerves that cool-off time and time-out are the best short-term measures. Teachers, and students, should not have to tolerate back-to-back disruption or hostile or aggressive behaviours directed to person or property. It is an essential feature of a classroom discipline plan (and of behaviour recovery in particular) that class teachers are *supported* by having a well planned time-out process.

Time-out policy

These key questions should be answered collaboratively by staff within a whole-school staff policy on time-out.

1   What sorts of behaviours would we normally expect to use time-out for?

2   How can we utilise time-out within the classroom?

3   When we exit for time-out what is the best way we can do it?

4   What if the child refuses to go? What is our support plan? (See p. 85.)

5   Where does the child go?

6   What happens to the child when he gets to the time-out place? (Do we use a colleague's room for time-out, a special time-out room or area, or the deputy principal's office?)

7   What is required of the child before coming back to his home classroom?

The essential feature of time-out (at any level) is that it gives the child (and the teacher?) time to cool down after a significantly disruptive incident and regain some self-control. All the children in the class need to know that cool-off time will be carried out when children make it difficult for others to feel safe, to learn, to be treated with respect. Time-out (and in-class cool-off time) is withdrawal time from the group until the child has settled and agrees to work by the fair rules. The professional discretion of what behaviour constitutes a significant breach of rights needs to be discussed and decided on by all staff so that time-out becomes part of a known process.

Staff, students and parents need to recognise that time-out is a consequence (not primarily a punishment). It should be designed and utilised so that the child sees a *connection* between his behaviour and the outcome (time-out). It is especially important for parents to understand what is meant by time-out so that they are not conjuring up images of standing in corners or sitting in some tiny cubicle!

Time-out is a short-term process that needs the back-up of other consequences and remediation processes. Time-out rarely, by itself, changes (though it may moderate) disordered behaviour. The key to the use of time-out is the employment of the certainty principle. Teachers don't need to yell at or drag the child heatedly out of the room. In fact the more dignity and calmness can be retained, the better. The message is, 'Whenever you act this way (be specific) this is what will happen'.

Time-out is not a reward; the child should not be asked why he did 'x', 'y' or 'z'. Nor should he receive counselling or special jobs or tasks *at that time*. Time-out ought to be as non-reinforcing as possible. I have had children kick and scream during time-out, but have not restrained them unless it is essential. I don't engage in many words, just the brief assurance that I'll 'release' them when they settle. The protocols of appropriate restraint when a child is a danger to himself or others needs to be discussed by staff. The child's return to the room should be carried out quietly, calmly, within agreed time schedules. For example, if a child goes to time-out twenty minutes before recess it may be appropriate to have him out *until* recess.

Cool-off time in the classroom

It may be appropriate to have a cool-off time in the room if the child is unduly unsettled and reserve exit/time-out (from the room) for the more significant rights-infringing behaviours. The main point is that children know the limits and expectations and connect their experience in time-out *to* the behaviour. This process is explained to all the children in the establishment phase of the year. That is, if they are making it difficult for others to learn or feel safe they will either be directed to work away from others for a period of time (relocation in the room), have some special (and non-reinforcing) cool-off time to settle and think about their responsibility, or be directed to leave the room until they are ready to work by the rules.

Give the child a directed choice (in effect a calm warning) wherever possible in the form of a reminder or choice (If . . . then . . .). It is pointless arguing or debating with students about their behaviour in front of an audience (it only feeds their attention-seeking or power-engaging behaviours). Some teachers use a special place in the room for cool-off time. The child is initially taken there with only a *brief* conditional reminder, 'When you've stopped feeling angry inside then you can come back to work at this table'. You need to make it clear that there is nothing wrong with the angry feelings but that when a child throws things around the table, or pushes, or pokes, or slaps then there is a logical consequence.

If there is an egg-timer placed in the cool-off area the student can come back on his own accord when he's settled and prepared to work within fair rules (a five minute egg-timer can be placed on a small table with a few cushions for the child to sit on).

It is crucial, though, that you carry out the whole process calmly; without yelling. A key management principle to remember here is that *the first person to calm in conflict is the teacher not the child.*

Supported exit and time-out

If the behaviour is seriously disruptive (i.e. safety or treatment rights being abused, or potentially abused, by the BD student) exit from the room provisions should be used. This, too, needs to be carried out calmly and decisively.

When I first began teaching I did some relief work in a number of difficult schools. I recall, on one occasion, a very testy Year 6 class. Within ten minutes one of the boys threw what was later described as a characteristic 'major wobbly'. He ran around the room several times and then hopped out of the window. I felt helpless partly because I didn't know what to do — I was unprepared — and also because I had no idea from senior staff that this (apparently typical behaviour) might happen.

Over the years I've come across countless situations like this where teacher stress, behaviour monitoring and protection of all students' rights could have been effectively handled within a whole-school approach to the use of time-out.

It is *generally* not advisable to have the student sitting outside the room as a form of time-out, especially BD students. This merely gives them an audience one door's length away! If the area just outside the door is used it should be for a short spell (five minutes) with a clear 'When . . . then . . . ' message as the parting words. 'When you've settled down then you're welcome to come back to your seat.' It is not advisable for staff who pass by such students in the corridor to question them (or talk with them) but rather to leave them in time-out mode.

Many BD students will not stand outside the room anyway, and some

will not even leave the room and go to the designated person or place. The direction to leave the room, will be resisted or simply provoke further acting out behaviour. In this case supported exit must be used.

Have a small red card (with the room number on) pinned to the wall or chalkboard. In a situation requiring exit from the room the card can be sent, with a reliable student, to either a nominated teacher, a senior teacher, or the deputy principal (this would all be planned ahead of time within the school's supportive time-out policy). One of the nominated teachers can then, on receipt of the card, go to that room and direct the child to 'Come with me now'. Another option that works well is to say (student's name) 'I'll see you in my office in a few minutes'. The exit process needs to be carried out calmly with an expectant tone.

On *rare* occasions even the presence of another teacher to direct the BD student away will meet a blatant refusal — the student sits down, or lies down and screams. On these occasions it is worth taking the whole class

out calmly and quietly, leaving their work. They can go for a walk around the building. This immediately removes the audience from the disruptive student long enough for him to connect that the audience has gone. The support colleague can then direct the disturbing student away to a time-out place. In small schools the support colleague is often teaching at the time their assistance is required. In this case the teacher who comes to exit will have to be spatially close so they can leave their class (with door open) to briefly walk across and escort the BD student back to their room.

Time-out, itself, may modify behaviour providing, of course, that time-out is not reinforced by talking sessions or lectures. Save counselling and recovery procedures for *another* time; actual time-out should be connected in the student's mind with withdrawal from his peer group and minimal over-servicing by the adult.

Classroom rotation

There needs to be a distinction made between having a student in a colleague's room to do set work there and the student going to a colleague's room when he is acting in a significantly disruptive way. Classroom rotation of the BD student can give the initiating class teacher a breather; this too is a planned process but it is different from time-out. If other teachers complain about the need for classroom rotation ('Why should I have *him* in my room for a whole period!') it is important to stress how they would appreciate that kind of support in the same situation. (They could be in that situation next year!) It goes without saying that forcing a classroom rotation process on staff is counter-productive; staff need to be encouraged not coerced.

The most important caveat

It is easy for me to write about positive discipline because I don't teach full-time any longer. However, I remember what it's like being 'boxed-in' with BD students day in, day out. I've been in unsupportive schools where the imputation of blame (covert) is on the teacher — that somehow the child's behaviour is the teacher's fault, or the parents' fault. I sometimes wonder how I would go at home with a child like that. In my more cynical moments I wonder how some senior staff would cope with BD students, or a 'reputation' class (the one no one wants!). How would they cope with little or no support?

Of course some teachers over-service attention-seeking behaviour. They 'buy into' power struggles, over-react to secondary behaviours, have dysfunctional beliefs. ('I'll *never* get anywhere with these students'; '*Nothing* I do matters!'; 'Students *should* respect me!'; 'He *should* do what I say the first time!'; 'He *shouldn't* answer back.') But failure, even stupidity, doesn't *make* teachers failures. It describes the human condition.

Eight out of ten

Teachers are fallible. If they get any of the skills mentioned in this book right, on an eight out of ten average they're doing brilliantly. That leaves them a reasonable fallibility ratio. Tiredness, frustration ('Will he *ever* learn!') and the often relentless pressure does wear anyone down. The important thing is an awareness matched with effort and backed-up with colleague support. If teachers plan to balance positive correction, within thoughtful preventative follow-up and remediation processes they will have done their best. And, if they shout, yell or 'lose the plot', they need to forgive themselves and simply (without sycophancy) apologise and rebuild the working relationship between the individual student, or class.

Students can forgive. It's when teachers do not make the effort to plan for management and discipline; when they merely over-react to disruptive behaviour that students find it hard to accept (or forgive). Much more disturbing is the teacher (or parent) who appears to take calculated satisfaction in putting children down, using the snide remark, public shaming, or persistent criticism.

In a supportive school environment teacher fallibility (like that of the students) is accepted. With that acceptance they feel better, they do better.

7   *Managing Anger*

*A*nger is a powerful emotion. At times of high frustration it can easily overtake rational control, even in adults. The exhibition of anger in children expressed in hostile ways towards furniture, property and person is difficult to manage and can be quite disturbing to teachers creating anxiety, confusion, even counter-anger.

It is important to consider any emotional pathology contributing to the child's expression of anger and aggression at school. This needs to be explored with the family and with due assistance from professional support services. The welfare of the class teacher and the other students also needs consideration. If the student's anger pathology is resistant to several months of teaching appropriate behaviours it will be necessary to look at alternative 'off-site' options for the student.

Emotion and expression

It is important to distinguish between the emotion of anger and its expression, and between anger and aggression. Anger is not bad per se; it often results from natural, even justifiable, frustration about situations that are difficult, stressful, unfair or unjust. Managing the emotion in a constructive way is not easy, indeed many writers have noted that a good deal of the world's problems are caused by the destructive outcomes of anger. Adults, therefore, should appreciate how difficult it is for children to *develop* appropriate coping skills for anger and conflict resolution.

Males seem to be taught (by default as much as 'design') that aggressive expression of anger is legitimate in resolving frustration. Certainly in dysfunctional families hostile or aggressive outcomes of anger are common. Research on bullying has shown that there is a correlation between family

'style' and aggressive behaviour (Olweus in Rubin & Pepler 1989; Smith & Thompson 1991).

BD children, especially, find it difficult to manage frustration and tend to have low frustration tolerance. They tend to be excited in less than helpful ways by their class peers thus reinforcing the BD child's attention-seeking behaviour. If they have a predisposition towards aggressive behaviour they also tend to be 'quick-responding' in social situations. Dodge (1981) observed that aggressive boys misattribute — have a biased attribution — in social settings. They *selectively attend* to the social cues of their peers putting the worst construction on these cues. Having an expectancy that a peer will be hostile, this biased attribution is self-reinforcing often resulting in retaliatory aggression (unless it is a bully–victim setting).

Behaviour recovery will need to address the child's:

- expectancy (which may include maladaptive thinking)
- selective attention to 'hostile' cues or perceived hostile cues ('He stared at me! — that meant he wants to fight!')
- biased weighing on those cues reinforced by (again) maladaptive thinking ('He hates me'; 'He's a _____'cos he looks at me.')
- behavioural alternatives

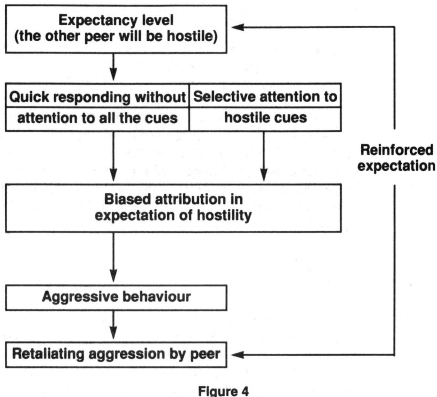

Figure 4
After Dodge (1981)

Learned aggression

Researchers have also shown that the frequency and kind of emotional reaction arising with anger is affected by cognition (Eron 1987; Meichenbaum 1977; Bernard & Joyce 1984). Aggressive behaviour is not merely the manifestation of some innate drive (or inborn testosterone that is predominantly male!). Aggression is also a learned behaviour. Male children *learn* to think, believe and act aggressively in our society. They learn early that conflict is more readily (and even acceptably) settled by aggressive means. (Macoby & Jacklin 1974, 1980).

Smith and Thompson (1991), Slee (1992) have shown that with attitude change, whole-school policies, clear consequences for bullies, reparative approaches for bullies, support and assertion skills for victims, education of students about non-violent conflict resolution, training of peer mediators, and positive discipline practices, the level of bullying and aggressive behaviour can be significantly reduced. Olweus, in his writing on bullying, has said that the next generation needs to be educated to manage anger constructively. This is the responsibility of school and parents in partnership.

School attitudes about aggression and bullying behaviour need to be clarified. 'Boys will be boys . . .', 'It's always been with us', 'It's character building', are just some of the damaging attitudes that perpetuate and 'tolerate' aggression (Rogers 1993b). There should be a *whole-school policy focus* clarifying the difference between normal quarrels and 'rough' play, and aggressive behaviour — particularly bullying. Repeated, selective, intentional hurting exercised over someone weaker should never be tolerated. There needs to be clear, unambiguous consequences for such behaviour; clear protection and due support process for the victim (with opportunities to facilitate meetings between bully and victim at the victim's request). Indeed the degree of support for the victims of aggression in a school is often correlated to the degree of bullying in that school (Slee 1992; Rigby & Slee 1993).

Teaching about anger

Children need to be taught that anger is a feeling. It is not bad to *feel* angry, it's what is done with the anger that counts. Especially important is the resolution of conflict in non-aggressive ways that still allow for an expression of appropriate frustrations. For example, people should get angry at injustice; what is done with that emotion, however, will determine how effectively some resolution about the injustice is achieved. It is worth noting here, that teachers can have a powerful role in feeding or reducing aggression. I have seen teachers snatch objects from children, yell at them in front of their peers, 'put them down', call them names, invade their personal space and wonder why the child reacts aggressively (verbally or physically). If teachers are angry with children it is better to model the behaviour they are seeking to teach them using these strategies:

- address the behaviour (without attacking the person)
- explain feelings in a clear way without denying frustration or anger (using 'I' statements or 'When/then')
- allow cool-off time when too upset to deal effectively with conflict in the heat of the moment

Children (and adults!) can learn that assertion is a way of making their point clearly and as unambiguously as possible. 'I feel upset (or annoyed, or angry) because you push in line instead of waiting' or 'When you push in line I feel annoyed (concerned, upset) because . . .' Aggressive anger should be saved for self-defence.

Children can learn what they get angry over; what is worth getting angry about; what they say to themselves when they get angry and after

they get angry. They need to be taught (especially through modelling) a vocabulary of anger. There is a difference between annoyed, frustrated, restless, panicky, irritated, displeased, uptight and angry.

Anger diaries

There is a difference in the degree of frustration or anger. A feeling thermometer or an anger diary can help measure this. Anger diaries can be a useful way of helping children (and teachers) learn what situations or circumstances trigger anger. When people become more aware of their anger arousal they are more likely to be able to manage it. If teachers can learn to recognise the triggers to children's anger they may be able to discern what is happening and then distract or divert in the short term. Appropriate use of humour, for example, can be a marvellous defuser in tense situations. Anger diaries can include a drawing of a thermometer that notes the degree of anger felt and what situations are causing it (degrees of mild or 'not very' through to 'I've blown it!' — out of control). Children need help with filling these in initially, but can use them in a self-directed way. With small children a picture diary with four stages of anger arousal shown can be used (see *Supplementary Material* PM 18).

I often use the word 'angries' (I point to my tummy and head) to describe the feeling of anger. Then I discuss what can be done when the 'angries' are there. This awareness assists the student in identifying the arousal and the situations which make him angry. He might assume that the stares of others or their refusals to play mean he is no good, or that he is stupid or they hate him. Even if he believes he is stupid, it doesn't *make* him stupid. You can make it clear to him that you like him (as do others) but you don't like these kinds of *behaviours* (be specific) that may also be causing others to 'reject' him.

These diaries can be used to discuss the anger triggers with the child (this is best done daily with children who display frequent anger outbursts). Initially you will need to virtually fill it in for him until he gets used to you connecting situations with the pictures. In recovery sessions you can then discuss what you have noticed about his 'angries', where they come from, and what he can do about it.

Developing an anger management plan

While it is OK to be angry there are some behaviours (arising from poorly handled anger) that are unacceptable. These behaviours need to be explained clearly to the child — even modelled if appropriate:

- throwing furniture, equipment
- pinching, punching, 'stabbing' with pencils
- elbowing, biting, regular 'stomping', or kicking, spitting in temper
- regular use of verbal aggression, and swearing at others

Verbal aggression can be overt (towards others or inanimate objects!) or covert to self as maladaptive self-talk. Again, it is the frequency, intensity and duration of these behaviours that is the cause for concern. Behaviour recovery can teach alternatives to these actions so that children know that when they get angry they can do other (specifically planned and rehearsed) behaviours instead.

Of course it is the *characteristic* behaviour, not the isolated incident, that needs to be addressed. Not all the above behaviours stem from anger. They may arise from attention-seeking or trying to exercise power over others; children who try to show peers and the teacher that no one can make them behave! Kicking furniture, hitting out at others, screaming and throwing tantrums are not acceptable. While teachers can understand that some children will deal with their emotions in this way it is important, for the rights of all, to set a safety context with limits, consequences, understanding and the teaching of alternatives.

Share with the child your own understanding of anger to help him tune into his experiences. 'Have you noticed what happens when you get angry?

When I get angry I sometimes close my fists like this. My neck goes stiff. I frown and I breathe funny.' A bit of mirroring can be helpful here. 'Have you noticed anything like that when you get angry? Can I tell you what I've noticed when you get angry?'

'I've noticed, Matthew, that you often get angry (show him the angry face on the diary) when you *can't* do the work (or whatever). I've noticed, too, that you clench your fists and breathe like this. Do you know I get angry too sometimes. I can understand how you feel that way. When I get angry my shoulders tense (model), my brows (see here) go in; my fists go tight (like this). But I've learned that *when* I get angry I can relax my neck muscles by doing this. I take four breaths. I relax my neck, my shoulders and back. I relax my fists and arms and my eyes. I also tell myself that I can relax, that it's not worth getting angry just because I can't do something or get something I want. After I've relaxed I try again, and I feel better.' This sharing helps build rapport. We can invite the child to make an anger plan. Invite him to practise simple 1, 2, 3 relaxation (see *Supplementary Material* PM 12).

The language of choice

A central tenet of behavioural responsibility is the emphasis placed on choosing behaviour — both negative and positive in outcome. Children need to learn that they are making choices — no one is actually *making* them throw furniture, or scream, spit or kick. This is a difficult concept to convey, but an essential one. Once teachers accept and treat children as if they can't help being aggressive in this way they do them a great disservice. They need to be treated on the basis that they are making choices. If the student refuses offers of assistance to understand his behaviour and make a plan he still needs to be treated as if that is his choice. Nor is he helped with threats — he is feeling those angry feelings. Denying it, or telling him to deny it, won't help.

Choosing behaviour means choosing consequences as well. Behavioural responsibility includes the ability to predict the consequences. Behaviour recovery includes teaching the child to think about 'What will happen if and when . . . ?' Remind the student again that his behaviour is his 'choice'; you (as his teacher) can help him make better choices for better outcomes. It is important that the child be allowed to choose (his consequences) even if he says he 'doesn't care!' Letting him know, in advance, the consequences of his present aggressive behaviour will help. Consistency in the application of consequences throughout the recovery process is most important.

Thinking and feeling

Older primary age children can be taught the relationship between thinking, feeling and behaviour. Angry or frustrated behaviour often relates to what is thought and believed. Strong feelings of anger also relate to what people believe and say to themselves about situations and circumstances. This message can be taught to older children using recovery-type teaching approaches. Using cartoon-type pictures and some brief mirroring (see p. 25 and *Supplementary Material* PM 13) you can show how angry thoughts and angry self-talk can often make the student feel worse — especially if he keeps saying those angry things, or negative things, over and over.

One way to illustrate the link between thought, emotion and action is to mirror the self-talk aloud while acting in an angry way. For example, say 'I can't stand it!' aloud while you throw the books on the floor, push furniture or slam the door. If you suspect the child might be intimidated in any way by such mirroring you can *generalise* the behaviour by saying 'Some children do this when they get angry', or by simply asking his permission. 'Can I show you what I mean? Can I show you what some children say inside their head when they get very angry?' or 'I'd like to show you ... OK?' You can then show how a different kind of self-talk can help the child do better and feel better when he gets angry.

Again, using cartoons with think bubbles (see *Supplementary Material* PM 14) you can illustrate the difference between thoughts that help and thoughts that make things worse. Think bubbles can contain self-talk such as 'This work is dumb!'; 'I hate this class!'; 'I can't stand it!'. It is useful to ask the child 'Are these thoughts helping thoughts or thoughts that will make things worse' or 'What might happen if a person *keeps* thinking these kinds of thoughts each time something hard or unpleasant happens?' Everyone gets upset, annoyed, irritated ... but how upset they become is affected by what they normally say inside their heads at the time they feel under pressure. This message — that emotions and the degree of stress felt is affected by beliefs as well as the event — is a difficult one for adults, let alone children (Bernard & Joyce 1984). What you're trying to teach the child is that he can learn to take some control over how bad he feels by learning to tune-in to his self-talk and use appropriate thought stoppers. 'Hey the work is not dumb — it's just hard. I can do it with my plan.' Thought stoppers can also help in self-prediction of consequences. 'If I keep saying this to myself, I'll feel worse — I might even end up in trouble.'

Modifying negative self-talk won't eliminate bad feelings but the child won't feel as bad about the situation. It is another tool which increases the sense of self-control.

Distracting himself from a stressful situation can be taught as a strategy for a child with low frustration tolerance: moving to another place to work

in the classroom, doing an alternative task for a while, going to see a teacher on playground duty when feeling angry. The possibilities can be discussed during recovery sessions emphasising that these options are not to be abused. One common self-distracting approach for older children is self-imposed time-out (SITO). The student contracts with you to leave the room for five minutes to sit in a safe place and cool down and to do this only if he feels the pressure 'to blow' is getting too strong. As part of a plan for anger management the 'leaving' can be left to the student's discretionary owner-ship. The viability of this approach needs to be discussed with colleagues and discarded if abused by the student. It has, however, been used very successfully by many teachers.

Teaching assertion skills to children is a common feature of social skills programs. It is not only non-assertive children who need such skills; overly hostile or verbally aggressive children need to learn the difference between being aggressive and being assertive. This is where modelling by the teacher is so powerful in clarifying the difference. By setting up common situations where assertive responses are appropriate and then practising the words and gestures, students can learn to observe social cues more carefully and not read aggression into every bump, encroachment of personal space or 'touchy' interpersonal responses. Trite as it sounds, an adequate program of physical activity for normal energy expression is useful for such children.

One of the goals of behaviour recovery is the enhancement of the BD student's self-esteem *within his classroom group* by gaining peer acceptance. By teaching the student how to relate non-aggressively (so he doesn't punch the student who takes or 'steals' his pencil without asking) teachers are increasing the likelihood of peer approval and social belonging.

Because a child's aggressive behaviour is often a badly focused (and habituated) way of belonging it is important that the classroom group dis-cusses how aggressive behaviour makes them feel. Many schools use class-room meetings as a forum in which students can learn to express their feelings and concerns in an open and assertive way and also to learn how to solve problems, cooperate with and help one another, without resorting to aggression (see p. 71). When *characteristically* aggressive children hear their peers talking about behaviour they don't (and do) like, such peer disap-proval can have (in itself) a salutary effect. The teacher can then guide the discussion to work out solutions and propose skills sessions where students can learn to relate to one another without easy and quick recourse to unnecessary aggression.

Bullies

Bullies are found in every age group (I have 'colleagues' who bully others) and they learn early that their behaviour gets them what they want. Like aggression, bullying is a learned behaviour (Besag 1989).

Bullies accept hostility and aggression as part of their world and use such means to gain their sense of belonging or peer popularity, maintain group leadership and influence others by threat to act, or relate to them in a way that satisfies their quest for 'relational power'. Most bullying in schools is psychological bullying but it is none the less distressing for those who are victim to such behaviour. Children who bully are less empathetic to the feelings of others (Smith & Thompson 1991) having little affectional monitoring of their own behaviour. They tend to be limited in their moral reasoning believing that it is the likelihood of punishment that determines any 'wrongness' in their behaviour. The crime is in being caught, not how their behaviour is affecting the rights and needs of others. Indeed this is the hardest truth to get through to bullies; in their distorted idiosyncratic logic they often believe their victims deserve to 'get done' because of the way they look, act, talk ('It serves them right').

Bullying is forcing others to do, act and feel the very things a bully would never want done to him. Bullying is not accidental, it is learned.

Bullying means:

•	courage	→	translates as	→	coercion
•	personal fear	→	is directed into	→	others being frightened
•	anger	→	is replaced by	→	aggression
•	personal inadequacy	→	is transferred into	→	an abuse of power
•	fun	→	is replaced by	→	hurting others for pleasure
•	personal suffering	→	is transferred	→	into causing others suffering
•	a bully's game	→	becomes	→	a nightmare for the victim
•	power	→	is	→	abused

Their victims:

- are smaller, weaker, different (in looks, speech, background, friendship, strength)
- are less able (or unable) to directly defend themselves
- have low self-esteem
- are likely not to tell or do anything except confirm the bully's 'world view'. (An abuse of relational power gets you what you want.)

There needs to be clear, school-wide consequences for bullying behaviour. Without clear consequences for such behaviour the bully continues in his (learned) belief that he can get his own way with impunity (Olweus 1978). Such consequences need to be set within a due process for dealing with bullying behaviour and an educational and policy context that emphasises rights-respecting behaviour. These consequences will be:

- known in advance and published in a school-wide policy document
- explained in relation to what the school means by bullying (see p. 94)
- discussed within classroom meeting time, during the establishment phase of the year and at times when the school experiences any spate of bullying behaviour

The normal features of consequences also apply; particular behaviour leads to certain, rather than severe consequences. This is hard. My own feeling about bullies has often been, 'I'd like to give them the same as they give to ...' This action would briefly ameliorate my strong feelings, no doubt, but merely confirm the student's warped world view.

Like any use of consequences on serious behavioural issues planning and policy direction needs to be established from a collaborative basis.

Dealing with bullies

It is important to have a due process for dealing with bullies that is consistent with the school's policy on behaviour management. This due process needs to embrace both consequences and, where possible, some form of behaviour recovery.

1   Isolate the bully for a formal meeting with a senior teacher. If there are several bullies within a gang it is better to deal with them one by one.

2   You should explain to the student/s what you know about the bullying: 'I need to talk to you because I've heard (or know) you've been saying (or doing) to ...' Name the victim and be as specific as possible about the bullying behaviour (Pikas 1991).

3   The ideal situation, of course, is direct knowledge of the bullying; often the knowledge is 'second-hand' or (sometimes) from the victim. It is important to check the bully's version of events: 'What do you know about this?' (again be as specific as possible). 'What has been happening?' Encourage the bully to talk about it. It is hard to remain calm with such students and, where there is no direct knowledge, it is important to avoid rushing the dialogue or using open interrogatives. 'Why did you do it?' Closed interrogatives are more effective ('What happened?', 'What did you say?', 'How many times?', 'When?')

4   Ask them 'How the victim (name) might feel when ...' Mirroring the behaviour can often establish some visual and emotional rapport, clarifying to the bully what his bullying behaviour looks and 'feels' like.

5   Refer to the school's rules about safety and respect and consequences of behaving in ways that hurt others' rights. Explain to him what it

means to bully others and why it is wrong. If the bullying is physical, involving other students, you can use the term assault and explain how people can be 'charged with assault'. Older students can be shown the school policy if necessary.

6 Make a plan or contract. Any plan needs to gain the bully's agreement about stopping such behaviour. Encourage him to come up with a

positive plan. ('What can you do to fix up your behaviour? What will you do so that (name victim) can feel safe now?')

If there has been a class meeting where the peer ethos is clearly against bullying explain, yet again, what his peers think about this kind of behaviour. ('What are some other ways we can be noticed, feel good in the group, enjoy having friends?') Explain and model the difference between aggression and assertion. ('What does it mean to legitimately stand-up for yourself (without hurting others on purpose)?') If they feel comfortable a plan for learning assertion may be useful.

Make sure any plan/contract is made clear to the student, get him to repeat it to you, and follow up in a week.

Keeping it simple, at the student's level of understanding, without introducing adult threats will help keep the focus on the *behaviour*. Explain why persistent name-calling, teasing, threats, racist language or physical hurting is wrong. No one *deserves* this. It is wrong, and it must stop. If he whinges about not liking 'x', 'y' or 'z' point out that while he does not have to like 'x', 'y' or 'z', he does have to respect them. Give some examples: 'Excuse me' instead of pushing in, using a fellow student's name instead of a nasty put-down name, asking to join in a game or borrow a bat or ball instead of barging in, spoiling or snatching.

It may be necessary for physically aggressive bullies to be isolated from social play for a period of time and have their playtime while others are inside. This means the bully still enjoys his right to playtime but isolated from his peers, with a teacher as a minder. It may also be necessary to have staggered home times for bullies if there is clear evidence of them threatening, extorting, or engaging in aggressive behaviour on the way to or from school. These approaches should be:

- explained to the parent/s
- explained as a related consequence not merely a punishment and be part of a counselling/contracting process
- designed to teach a connection between behaviour and outcome.

Bullies and relational power

Most children will quarrel, argue, challenge, even hit out at others when angry. They will exhibit these behaviours because of frustration, tiredness, crowded conditions, developmental considerations, provocation. These behaviours are not bullying. Bullying is selective, intentional, often secretive (accompanied by threats) and repetitive. Bullying can be psychological (teasing, racist or sexist slurs and accusations, put-downs, threats to do something) or physical and is often both. Boys are much more likely to use physical bullying!

Bullies are characterised by their abuse of relational power. All bullying is an exercise in power and control to the degree in which it satisfies the need to feel important and significant. It is one of the lowest routes to self-esteem. Bullies often come from dysfunctional families and have been bullied themselves, and a significant number go on to display traits of delinquency and to an engagement with the criminal justice system (four times more likely to do so according to a study by Eron 1987).

Everyone has some degree of relational power. Bullying is more than a misuse of this power (it is that); bullies abuse the exercise of power *socially*. While such behaviour is always present and displayed with monotonous regularity in politics, films and sit-coms, playgrounds, families, between nations, it cannot be excused on that basis. One of the factors likely to perpetuate bullying in schools is the attitudes that endorse it. 'Boys will be boys', 'It's always with us you'll never stop it!', 'It's character-building.' Bullying is wrong (even if 'always with us') because it acts against the fundamental right of students to feel safe at school and to be treated with respect (Rogers 1993b). Bullying is also perpetuated by the code of silence about such behaviour where students believe that to tell is to 'dob'. One way to work on the issue at school is to raise bullying in a creative studies unit (art, media, stories, drama) to allow expression, exploration and action planning. Bullying is best dealt with by a whole-school approach, not by a 'let sleeping dogs (or bullying dogs) lie' approach. If recent research by Rigby and Slee (1993) is any indication, schools have a major behavioural concern to address. One child in twenty engages in persistent bullying, one child in eight is continually victimised to the extent it affects his school life.

A whole-school approach

Smith and Thompson (1991) have outlined features of 'low-bullying' and 'high-bullying' schools. The most significant factor in distinguishing between the two is the degree to which teachers and administrators have firmly held views about the unacceptability of bullying and have a whole-school policy in place to address it. This policy should involve all staff and students and as many parents as possible. Other features of low-bullying schools include the degree to which victims are taken seriously, listened to, allowed to tell their story without the brush-off, and the certainty that due process will follow the incident. For example, in the playground where most bullying occurs (because it's harder to be seen) victims should at least be listened to ('I'm glad you felt you could tell me') and then a follow-up organised with the class teacher.

The school's educational program should address protective behaviours and what it means to enjoy the right to feel safe. For example, rather than merely having an anti-bullying program, it is more effective to develop a positive behaviour program *within which* bullying behaviour is addressed. What are the behaviour management practices of staff — generally speaking? Is there a correlation between bullying (verbal bullying) by teaching staff and the tacit acceptance by children of such behaviour?

If teachers utilise public shaming, undue (and persistent) criticism, put-downs, intentional embarrassment and sarcasm, aggressive (rather than assertive) management styles then such modelling will clearly have an effect and easily override any policy statement about self-discipline and respect for mutual rights!

School policy should outline what bullying is, the due process taken when bullying is reported, how victims and bullies are treated, contact procedures with parents, and the educational overlap with the school's rights, responsibilities, rules and consequences. The school can address bullying in a range of ways.

1   Education can raise awareness of what bullying is, how people feel when it happens, what can be done about it. Drama, role-playing, story-telling and classroom meetings are ideal vehicles for exploring the issues at stake. Both bullies and victims can see themselves as others see them and hear what their peers believe needs to be done. Education is especially important in creating an environment that endorses 'It's OK to tell if someone keeps on doing . . .' Classroom meetings can explore how this can be done confidently. The student community can increase the sense of social security when it corporately views bullying as wrong.

2   It is important to establish a due process for assisting victims and addressing bullies.

3   Clear consequences for bullying need to be outlined to the students. These can include isolation, partial withdrawal from playtimes, supervision.

4   Contact with parents is crucial but the school will need to outline how it will do this in a non-judgemental and supportive way. Having a clear policy, with a published due process, will help the communication between home and school.

5   'Safe areas' at playtimes (library, art room, alternative programs) need to be created.

6   Peer arbitrator programs can assist. A child can go to a peer arbitrator trained in mediating (they normally wear a badge or hat or are well known to students).

7   Victims and bullies need to learn to behave differently using the approaches outlined in this text. *Teaching* behaviour change on a one-to-one basis can help develop these skills.

Peer involvement

One of the schools I worked in had signs up for a while, of a bully face with a 'no' line through it and the acronym DOB. It had a two-way meaning: 'Don't obey bullies' and 'Dob on a bully' (tell teachers about bullying when and where it is happening). It proved successful. They also held a number of classroom meetings across the school to deal with the Australian cringe about 'dobbing' and tale-telling that it is basically wanting to get someone else into trouble, or pay them back or get lots of attention from the teacher or other students. Asking for help or support from the teacher is not dobbing; letting a teacher know when several students are ganging up on others, or threatening them, or using racist put-downs repeatedly to taunt is not dobbing; letting a teacher know when the threat merchants are abusing toilet privileges is not dobbing — *it's putting those who can help in the know.* Classroom meetings, with a consideration of specific questions, are a positive vehicle for clarifying this issue with children. 'How does this behaviour affect you directly? In what way does it work against others' rights? What can we do?'

Protective behaviour programs have taught children that 'Nothing is so bad that we can't tell', 'Nothing is so bad that something can't be done about it'. Teachers need to be careful not to lightly dismiss reports by victims or observers. If you suspect that a victim (or observers) are 'ambiguous' or out for revenge then you'll need to check with your colleagues to get a rounded picture. However, children should be encouraged to tell if the bullying doesn't stop.

Helping victims

I have worked with many adults in the workplace who have recounted being bullied who felt (and believed) that they were powerless to do anything and worse it was 'somehow their fault'. At school, victims (unless they are the 'bully-turned-victim') tend to be loners, reluctant to tell and have low self-esteem in terms of successful adaption to the social world. (A person can be a loner and still be successful in terms of social adaption.) Loners who are victims tend to play alone, have limited and poor social network skills, and exhibit an unhappiness exacerbated by poor social networking, lack of positive friendships and the bullying itself.

When a victim reports being bullied take them seriously; genuine victims need to be believed. Encourage them to talk about what has happened. Stay calm and avoid over-reacting. Strangely our over-reaction (as parents or teachers) may see them 'clam up' and resist any supportive action or plan we might offer. Listen carefully and help them to be as specific as possible. When? Where? How? Whom? How often? This is the hardest part; encouraging them to talk and getting a clear picture. If students do not report anything but the suspicion of bullying is there, a one-to-one talk with the child about bullying may well be in order. 'It's OK to talk about it if it ever happens to you.' As with all one-to-one sessions ethical probity is essential especially with male teachers and female victims. The safest approach is to raise the issue of silent victims with colleagues and plan a meeting with the child based on colleague advice and the policy guidelines.

Bullying may be occurring when students regularly complain of losing things or missing belongings. They may have bruises they won't talk about, or don't want to go out at lunch-time or recess. Is the child overly withdrawn? Frequently complaining of pains (headaches, stomach aches)? Has the student lost interest in school work? These observations should not be lightly dismissed especially when reported by parents. The ideal situation is to work with the parents to develop a range of positive, supportive strategies.

Strategies for victims

Victims of bullying need reassurance, they want to be believed and supported. Most of all they want the bullying to stop. Encouraging them to tell who is doing it can enable you to then work with the bully/bullies as well. The following strategies are used widely in schools, often in combination. As well as stopping the bullying in a particular instance you need to teach the victim strategies for dealing with bullies wherever they are.

1   Children should be encouraged to play with others rather than alone. One school used a classroom meeting approach to raise the issue of children having and complaining of no one to play with. Two classes held concurrent meetings to discuss ways of making sure 'we all had someone to play with'. The most novel suggestion was that anyone who didn't have someone to play with should sit on the seats underneath the flagpole in the playground. If anyone was sitting there someone from one of the classes would go up and invite them to play. It worked.

2   A minder can be employed for a while along the lines of the plan helper idea (see p. 59).

3   If a bully threatens a child he can say straight away that 'Mr/Mrs _____ knows about what you've been doing and saying. If you touch me (or my bag, my food, my bike) I'll report it'. This, at least, lets the bully know that adults are aware of what is happening. They may think twice and weigh up the consequences. It is also important to recognise that,

for children, persistent minor harassment (taking property without asking or giving back, kicking someone else's schoolbag around, is quite stressful). It is important to deal with this at the classroom and duty-of-care level (wet-day supervision, playground). If staff are seen to give up their time and get to the facts and take action, as fairly as possible, students are more likely to report, feel supported, and also believe that support is available in more major aspects of bullying (Smith & Thompson 1991).

4   All teachers should follow through and report bullying incidents wherever they occur in the school. Even those victims who are bullies and become prey to others who are stronger need support and guidance rather than a mere, 'It serves you right'.

5   Classroom meetings connected with themes such as being safe in the playground and bullying can be run. Children can discuss the following questions.

- What do we mean by bullying?
- What sort of people bully others?
- Where does it normally occur?
- Why do you think people bully others?
- What do they get out of it?
- How can we stop bullying?
- What sort of things would be helpful to say?
- What should we do if we see bullying happening?
- How could we report bullying?
- What should happen to bullies?

These meetings can also discuss the difference between what students should try to handle themselves when hassled, how they can work cooperatively to settle differences, and how to report to teachers when it's getting too much. Students need to balance the difficult realities of (i) there won't always be a teacher there, or an adult, when they're being hassled, teased, put down, threatened, excluded, or even hurt by bullies and (ii) they have a right to feel safe, be treated with respect, and it's OK to tell.

6   A skills program can be organised across the school which focuses on the difference between students standing up for their rights to feel safe and treated with respect and learning to handle the bullies of this world with confidence. Indeed confidence is as much a skill as a state of mind. Students with low self-esteem can be encouraged to undertake any activity that will increase their risk-taking such as interviewing others for a project or speaking in front of the class (Borba & Borba 1982; Cranfield & Wells 1976; McGrath & Francey 1993).

7   If the victim is willing it can be useful to confront the bully (bullies) with the support of a teacher. A meeting is set up with the bully and victim (and the adult facilitator). The victim explains to the bully (bullies) what it is they are doing and that they want this bullying (be specific) to stop. The effect it is having should be described briefly. The bully then has to agree it will stop and be specific about what he will do.

It is important that the tone of such a meeting be calm and positive without denying the seriousness of such behaviours. Key questions can be asked.

- What happened?
- Why do you think it happened (or has been going on)?
- What rule or right is affected?
- What can we (you) do to stop it?

It is also important at such a meeting that the facilitator encourage the bully (bullies) to answer the questions in their own words. If the bullying is concerned with physical aggression, or threats of same, the bully needs to be reminded that this is assault and serious. The consequences for such behaviour will need to be spelled out. Of course this process can be carried out with the victim and bully (bullies) separately but there is value (if the victim is confident enough) in addressing the bully face-to-face with teacher support. If these meetings are held separately it can still be useful to get the bully and victim together so that the victim can hear the bully say that his behaviour will stop.

Teaching assertion

Assertion is first and foremost a skill. It is a way of making a person's needs and rights known without trampling on the rights of others. It is a skill needed by both the bully and the victim. Using the program approach outlined in Chapter 3 the class teacher (or support teacher) can set up a number of one-to-one teaching sessions to outline the need for this skill, practising it (using role-play similar to the setting in which it will be needed), and getting feedback from the student as they use it in the 'natural setting'.

While bullying is never right there are some victims whose interpersonal behaviours may unfortunately highlight behaviours that bullies seem to pick on:

- being a loner, playing alone
- a whine in the voice
- lowered hang-dog look
- non-confident body posture
- hunched-over shoulders

- skewed, darting, uncertain eye-contact
- hands hung low, passive stance

Children who look like this do not look as if they are in control. While this is not their fault, it presents an unfortunate picture to the child's peers. The reality is that they are more likely to be picked on than other students. Explain why you are having this meeting time. 'When people pick on you, tease . . . there won't always be others there to help, so I want to show you a plan that will help you, OK?' Using mirroring techniques you can model the sorts of behaviours above and ask the student, 'What do you think others feel when *we* look (here the teacher models) and speak like this?' Then you can invite them to make a plan, to take charge of their behaviour.

1   Help the student understand how he presents to others. 'What does your behaviour look like, sound like? Do you know?' (Use mirroring here.)

2   Explain to the child that when he 'takes charge', he can learn to speak and behave and feel differently; stronger and without so much fear.

3   Set up a scenario similar to the situation the child experiences using picture cues and modelling techniques (off-task and on-task behaviours related to non-assertion and assertion).

4   Model the new behaviour: look strong, think strong, say strong, walk away.

Positive ignoring

You should explain to a victim that sometimes it's OK to walk away (walk tall) from teasing and name-calling. It's a good idea, though, for him to walk away towards a teacher or to some students with whom he feels safe. In the one-to-one sessions you can encourage the child to practise walking tall, walking away, while the simulated teasing is going on. Positive ignoring: 'The names can't really hurt me unless I believe they can. Inside my head I am still OK'. Part of each teaching session can address self-talk (see p. 48).

Again, it can be useful to make up a practice card for this self-talk (see *Supplementary Material* PM 15a, 15b, 16). If the parents are supportive this can be practised at home as well as at school. Then next time a student says or does the bullying behaviour the child can:

- turn and face the bully
- look into his eyes
- speak into his eyes

- stand tall, head up without smiling
- tell them what it is he doesn't like without shouting or arguing and finish with a 'stop' statement
- walk away

If, in rehearsal, the student still adopts a non-assertive, whining voice, go over it again. 'Listen carefully and watch me.' (Model the whole sequence.) 'Now, have another go.' Encourage approximation towards the desired behaviour. It will take several goes before it connects. It can help to practise it 'out of simulation' first just like rehearsing a line in a play. Then do it in a simulated, face-to-face setting. You could ask him if he would like to practise it with a friend next time (a plan helper). Remember it will take time; children develop these postural, tonal behaviours and damaging beliefs over a period of time. It will (like any other skill) take practice, effort, feedback, and some success.

Remind him that if the bully continues with his behaviour, especially with threats of violence, it's OK to say: 'Mr (or Mrs) _____ knows about what's happening' then report it ASAP. At subsequent sessions go through the feedback questions (see p. 42) and refine the plan as needed.

Ambiguous victims

Some victims of bullying are themselves ambiguous when it comes to unin-vited teasing, name-calling or getting hit. They tease others, pick on them, 'stir' and hassle until they get a response (even being hit) then cry 'foul'. It is especially helpful if you have actually seen this happen. It happens in classrooms from time to time and is a form of attention-seeking for the victim.

- Avoid over-servicing the suspected victim. Stay calm and focus on the problem.
- Ask the victim what happened and what he could do in a similar situation next time. If he doesn't know, give him a plan that minimises adult intervention.
- If you know he is a 'teaser-cum-victim', explain that if he wants to keep getting hassled all he has to do is keep doing what he's doing.

If bullying is going to be addressed effectively it will require a whole-school approach that includes attitude change, policy direction, positive management practices, targeted education, adequate support for victims and behaviour recovery for *both* victims and bullies.

8 *Challenges of the Program*

*N*o program in itself, will solve the variety of problems presented by human behaviour. Behaviour recovery is an attempt to bring some balance to the rights and responsibilities of the BD student, his peers in the classroom and the class teacher. Like many programs it uses bits of paper to help structure complicated reality: cartoon plans, diagrams, memory aids, checklists but at the end of any piece of paper is a human being. It is the human *relationship* within which the difficult task of teaching new behaviour occurs. This relationship is tested, frequently, in any journey of behaviour recovery and, inevitably, there are particular challenges and problem areas that need to be recognised and addressed.

Teachers want to create a safe, rights-enhancing environment for all students; an environment that can increase the BD student's chance of success at school and beyond. It is important to recognise that while the school cannot compensate for this student's home background there is a lot which can be done at school.

Some teachers will complain about being involved in the program. 'Why should we spend all this time on one pain of a student!'; 'Why should I give up my time to cover another teacher's class so that (BD student) can have one-to-one attention?' These complaints can be answered by saying: 'It could be your son or daughter. How would you want them treated?'; 'You may have a student like this one next year!'; 'This is a whole-school effort — to support the class teacher and the BD student and his family.'

Teachers who don't have (or cannot sustain) the emotional reserves to give one-to-one time, or where the relationship is poor, will benefit from a colleague doing the behaviour recovery. What is essential though is that the class teacher's discipline and encouragement style is consistent with that of the support colleague.

It needs to be affirmed that the child is not 'getting away with anything'. The school is simply setting up a positive colleague support structure. The student faces the same corrective discipline as all students.

The program has less likelihood of success if teachers do not give colleague support in covering classes (for one-to-one recovery time); time-out; rotation of the student on bad days. The best support a teacher can get is someone taking the student off her hands for half a day to give her a breather, and 'enrolling' the BD child in another class for the morning or afternoon. This is not time-out but rotation time-out for the teacher. All support and relieving teachers must be aware of the plan (and progressive plans) so they can use the same approaches as the class teacher. This is essential if the plan involves playground behaviour.

Where there appears to be a large number of 'difficult' students as well as BD students (say up to 10 per cent of the class) teachers can:

- identify the most disturbing of the group and concentrate on him first
- work in pairs
- use a class-group reinforcement program where the class is divided into mixed ability groups and 'reward' schedules developed to enhance on-task social/academic behaviours (see Rogers 1990, Chapter 7)

Really 'hard-core' cases do respond to behaviour recovery approaches. However, there is a percentage who resist all attempts to be assisted in behaviour change. If that resistance, over time, is significantly affecting the rights of the other students (and the teacher) then a formal inquiry process will need to consider referral processes outside the school. This should be urged by the administration on advice of the class teacher in consultation with the caregiver/s.

Colleague support

The rationale for the specific teaching of behaviour needs to be explained to all staff, especially specialist staff. The discipline protocols and practices will need to be clarified so a *consistency of practice* is more likely. There are a number of crucial areas which must be considered.

- All specialist teachers should have a copy of any behaviour plans in use by the class teacher.
- The fundamental philosophy of the plan/s should be outlined (probably at a staff meeting or as the need arises).
- An agreed use of cool-off time, exit (especially the procedural aspects) and time-out measures should be decided on. Who is involved for

supported exit? How long should the student be out-of-class? Where does he go? (see pp. 85–8)

Specialist teachers need to be familiar with the language of discipline used by the class teacher. In a school with a whole-school approach to behaviour management this will be less of a problem. It is advisable that consequences for disruptive behaviour in specialist time (or playtime) be normally carried out by the duty-of-care teacher at that time. Even if deferred consequences are used the certainty-of-consequence principle is more likely to be realised if the duty-of-care teacher follows through with the necessary (related) consequence.

Working with parents

Any school working with BD students will often be in contact with parents. These 'meetings' should be as supportive as possible. Most parents will recognise that the school is doing its best and their support will be gained by being non-judgemental about their parent role. Their understanding and support for what is being done at school is very important.

There are some children whose disruptive behaviour patterns present from significant emotional pathology: trauma associated with family breakdown, emotional deprivation, anxiety about what is happening in the family, emotional, physical or even sexual abuse. Any suspicion of such preconditions affecting school behaviour needs to be dealt with through a team approach and specialist communication support extended to the family.

When explaining the behaviour recovery program it is important to stress the supportive nature of the program. Parents are not asked their permission for one-to-one withdrawal in class time, rather it is explained to them why this school program will help their child work more positively in class, enable him to perform better in his work and help him feel better about himself as a person. The focus should be on the positive aspects of the program without minimising the disruptive nature of their child's behaviour. Explain that this approach is used in many schools to enable students to recognise why their behaviour is a problem, and what they can do to learn positive behaviours.

Show parents the cards, explain what is entailed in one-to-one sessions, and discuss the possibility of utilising a classroom meeting approach (see Chapter 5). Explain that classroom meetings are the regular forum whereby the class can raise issues of concern and work on a plan of action within the fair rules. Invite their feedback about the use of such meetings to discuss social behaviour in the classroom.

Explain the use of time-out provisions when the child (any child, not

just theirs!) makes it difficult for others to learn, feel safe, be treated with respect. This should be explained within the context of the school's discipline policy. Point out the difference between punishment and consequence with respect to time-out. Emphasise throughout the *educational* features of the program and the goals of enhancing cooperative behaviours in (and out of) the classroom.

Set up regular meetings for feedback to parents; these meetings can include the student as well. Show them the progress (via the cards) and the comments which have been made in the running records. At one school (where parents were often rung up about their offspring's disruptive behaviour) the class teacher started to ring up about positive behaviours. Initially she got the following reply. '_____ (expletive)! What's he done now?'; 'Well Mrs _____, I just rang to say Damien's been working really well in maths today, especially . . .' Silence. Then a more measured, 'Oh, yes, well, thank you for calling'. Damien came to school next day. 'Hey, what did you say to me mum yesterday?' 'Why?' 'Well she was a bit happy about what you said.' Few parents object to the attempts by a school to assist their children with behaviour recovery. Some parents even take the ideas and apply them in the home environment.

If the parents are generally hostile to school, to 'authority figures', a due process should be set up that protects the class teacher from unauthorised visits. Inform them of the school's discipline policy and why behaviour recovery approaches are being used. Give them a summary of what the program is, in writing, and a copy of the school's discipline code. Again, keep the tone supportive where possible, assertive where necessary.

If the program is clearly not working and significantly disruptive behaviour is normative, the school will need to use sanctions such as suspension and pursue formal education department inquiry procedures.

The class teacher

The unique relationship that primary school teachers have with their students means that they are the ideal people to engage the child in the learning of behaviour. While a 'behaviour tutor' can quite comfortably utilise the tenets of teaching behaviour, the fact that a tutor does not spend (normally speaking) significant day-in, day-out time with a child may work against the frequent encouragement essential to any success. Furthermore, the link between modelling and rehearsal and what happens in the classroom is not as strong when a tutor is involved. So, wherever possible, support should be given to the class teacher to engage in a teaching behaviour program.

Behaviour tutors

There are some teachers who can (conceptually anyway) see the value of behaviour recovery approaches but are so jaded and stressed by recidivist behaviour they haven't got the emotional energy to give the program the attention it deserves. 'Look, I'm so fed up with him, I've had it. If I give the one-to-one time, even with the support offered, I feel I just couldn't be convincing with him!' In these cases it is counter-productive for the class teacher to conduct behaviour recovery sessions. A tutor can both assist and support the teacher to regain a sense of proportion and possibility for the child in question. Such support (when it breeds any successful change in the child's behaviour) may rekindle enthusiasm in the class teacher.

A tutor can develop the program in the same way as the class teacher as long as it is someone well-known to the class. Someone who has spent enough time with the students to be accepted as 'staff'. It can be a parent who is involved in learning support, a support teacher or school psychologist. What is crucial is that they are familiar with the program of teaching behaviour as outlined in this text and have available the one-to-one time necessary.

It goes without saying that anybody selected to tutor the child does so within a team approach, and that they work effectively with the class teacher. Part of their role is to increase the congruence between success in one-to-one sessions with the student and how the class teacher can build on the rehearsal of target behaviours. Such tutors need to demonstrate enthusiasm; even a sense of humour; the ability to communicate well and give positive feedback; a non-judgemental stance; willingness to 'hang in there' so they can spot even the small approximations made by the child towards positive behaviour. While this sounds like a lot to ask, these are skills possessed by any effective teacher.

There needs to be an agreement between the class teacher, administration support and the tutor as to how the tutor time fits in with an overall plan to assist the class teacher and the BD student. Of particular importance is the release time and how it will be organised. Protocols for releasing the child from class need to be clarified and an agreement made that the class teacher will be supportive of the program itself, each individual plan within the program, and the feedback necessary by the class teacher to encourage the BD student. This needs to be clarified from the outset. It is counter-productive if the class teacher does not follow up what the tutor has been doing. Especially important is the frequent encouragement of positive behaviour, and approximations, by the BD student, to his plan. It can be helpful if the tutor comes into the classroom on some occasions to model the quiet encouragement essential to behaviour recovery plans.

The class teacher, or tutor, and supervising teacher also need to clarify the discipline procedures used: non-punitive in style, simple brief reminders or directions using the plan as a focus, choices instead of threats and planned, related consequences known in advance. It will need to be emphasised that the BD child is not getting different discipline (it is the same as for the others), he is getting support outside the room to increase on-task and positive social behaviour in the room.

It is also important that the class teacher is not made to feel she is ineffective because a tutor is working with her. It is helpful, initially, if a supportive senior teacher can set up the teaming necessary to make the behaviour recovery initiative work. The emphasis ought to be that this is a whole-school initiative to enable BD students, the class, and the class teacher to provide the most adequate support possible. Part of the tutor's role ought to be to work with the class teacher in the classroom — as much as time release allows. It can be useful for the tutor to support the class teacher in conducting at least one classroom meeting (see p. 63) to focus on what the class can do about disruptive behaviour.

Training of tutors should involve:

- familiarity with the program material
- assistance in preparation of picture cue material
- regular evaluation of each recovery session with a senior supervising teacher
- discussion of the program with any other teachers (inside or outside the school) using recovery approaches for teaching behaviour
- understanding of time-out procedures (It will be necessary to clarify the use of time-out, in and out of the room, and how it can be utilised in a calm, non-argumentative fashion.)

Staying power

All BD children will have heard many negative or mixed messages, resulting from their frustrating behaviour. 'What's wrong with you, how many times have I told you not to call out in class?'; 'Why can't you put your hand up like everyone else?'; 'No, you can't do your painting now because you haven't cleaned up your play dough mess yet and I'm tired of telling you! When you leave the play dough out it gets hard and when it gets hard we can't use it, can we!' Negative messages, 'I'm sick of telling you!' interspersed with sarcasm or labelling ('idiot', 'stupid', 'dumb') have a self-fulfilling effect.

It takes staying power to encourage these children towards responsible behaviours, appropriate social belonging and increased self-esteem. As Downing (1986) wrote, one needs to 'see the potential in this child'. A combination of behaviour recovery, positive discipline, active encouragement, and teacher and peer support will help to attain this goal.

Defining success

It is important to consider what constitutes success of a program like behaviour recovery. Success can be described as a decrease in frequency, intensity and duration of disruptive behaviours with a corresponding increase in the on-task counterparts. I've worked with teachers who complain that, 'He *still* calls out when we're having story time.'; 'He *still* rocks in his seat.'; 'he *still* calls out for help in instruction time.' It is important to ask 'How many times now (since intervention) is he calling out, butting in, seat wandering?' A drop in frequency, hopefully a significant drop, has to be seen as a success. Some teachers think that all disruptive behaviour should cease in order to prove any success for an intervention program. This is clearly less than realistic, even well-behaved children are disruptive from time to time. Remember, too, that any child in behaviour recovery is not given special licence to be disruptive in school, he is being given special *assistance*. Normal disciplinary processes apply with children on these programs as with any children (correction, consequences, time-out, suspension).

Using journals, the contract cards, and colleagues' feedback (i.e. in specialist areas such as library lessons, art, music, physical education, playground), changes in behaviour can be timelined and assessed.

Behaviour recovery: an endorsement

It's very time-consuming, especially in the initial stages, but the question we had to ask as a staff was, 'What's going to be the most advantageous . . . in the long run'. Yes, it is time-consuming but we had to consider how best we could use our time with stretched resources. How could we balance the teachers' needs (and support) with the rights of the other students as well as the (BD) student.

Jim: school principal

Professional development

Many of the skills used by teachers in behaviour recovery are simply effective teaching and management skills. The fine-tuning of skills including running classroom meetings, positive discipline practices, use of encouragement, modelling and rehearsal need to be part of a school's on-going professional development.

These skills are best developed in a climate of colleague support. Teachers need the opportunity to talk about discipline concerns, to feel it's OK to share the angst that goes with managing BD students, to have genuine opportunities and appropriate forums for problem solving and planning workable remediation and time-out programs.

Conclusion

Essentially, behaviour recovery is a structured process within which a BD student can learn behaviours that will enable him to be more successful in behaviour and learning outcomes in school. It also aims, concurrently, to enhance positive self-esteem and the acceptance of personal responsibility. It is hoped, too, that the BD child will gain a more positive peer acceptance through modifying his behaviour and the creative use of classroom meetings.

Some children respond very quickly to behaviour recovery approaches, others will take a lot longer. If the support (or at least the understanding) of parents can be enlisted — even better. Schooling is a partnership between school and home and parents need to take some responsibility for their children's behaviour at school.

Behaviour recovery requires significant whole-school support and understanding if it is going to work. BD students spend a third of their day at school, most of it with the class teacher as caregiver. In fact, for some BD students school and their teacher may well provide a secure, sane place in their lives. At the end of the day it is this that will change disturbing disordered behaviour. It is the quality of human interaction that will enable the program to have any effect. BD students impose considerable strain on the limited resources of a school; there is no question that an increase in integration aides (or teachers) could be usefully allied to behaviour recovery training in schools.

There are few off-site units that primary age children can go to for specialist remediation and, in these days of integration into the mainstream (as the philosophic norm), schools are expected to take on almost every student. The fact is, anyway, that the number of BD students exceeds the availability of off-site units, except in extreme cases. Balancing the learning, welfare, and behavioural concerns of *all* students at school is not easy but programs like behaviour recovery can assist by enabling BD children to believe they can take positive control of their school experience.

Bibliography

Anderson, L.S. 'The aggressive child', *The Best of set Discipline*, ACER, Hawthorn, Victoria.

Bernard, M. & Joyce, M. 1984, *Rational Emotive Therapy with Children and Adolescents*, J. Wiley & Sons, New York.

Besag, V. 1989, *Bullies and Victims in Schools*, Open University Press, Milton Keynes, United Kingdom.

Borba, M. & Borba, C. 1982, *Self-esteem: A Classroom Affair*, vols 1 & 2, Dove Communications, Melbourne.

Braiker, H.B. 1989, 'The power of self-talk', *Psychology Today*, December, pp. 23–7.

Cranfield, J. & Wells, H.C. 1976, *100 Ways to Enhance Self-concept in the Classroom*, Prentice-Hall, New Jersey.

Dempster, M. & Raff, D. 1992, *Class Discussions: A Powerful Classroom Strategy*, Hawker-Brownlow Educational, Cheltenham, Australia.

Dodge K.A. 1981, Social competence and aggressive behaviour in children, paper presented to the Mid-western Psychological Association, Detroit, May.

Dodge, K.A. & Frame, C.L. 1982, 'Social cognitive biases and deficit in aggressive boys', *Child Development*, no. 53, pp. 620–35.

Donaldson, M. 1978, *Children's Minds*, Fontana Collins, Glasgow.

Downing, C.J. 1986, 'Affirmations: steps to counter negative, self-fulfilling, prophesies', *Elementary and School Guidance and Counselling*, no. 20, pp. 175–9.

Dreikurs, R. 1968, *Psychology in the Classroom: A Manual for Teachers*, 2nd edn, Harper & Row, New York.

Dreikurs, R. 1985, *Happy Children: A Challenge to Parents*, Fontana, Glasgow.

Ellis, A. & Bernard, M.E. (eds) 1983, *Rational-Emotive Approaches to the Problems in Childhood*, Plenum Press, New York.

Eron, L.D. 1987, 'The development of aggressive behaviour from the perspective of a developing behaviourism', *American Psychologist*, 5, pp. 435–42.

Grinder, M. 1991, *Righting The Educational Conveyor Belt*, Metamorphosis Press, Portland, Oregon.

Grinder, M. 1993, *(ENVOY) Educational Non-verbal Yardstick*, M. Grinder & Assoc., 16303 NE 250 Ninth St., Battleground, Washington.

Hall, J. 1993, *Confident Kids*, Lothian Books, Melbourne.

Harrison, J. 1991, *Understanding Children: Towards Positive Relationships*, ACER, Hawthorn, Victoria.

Hutchins P. 1990, 'Biological perspectives on behaviour problems: an essential consideration for practical resolution', in *Practical Approaches to Resolving Behaviour Problems*, (eds) S. Richardson & J. Izard, ACER, Hawthorn, Victoria.

Hyndman, M. & Thorsborne, M. 1992, Bullying: a school focus, paper presented to the Queensland Guidance and Counselling Association Conference, Queensland.

Kaplan, R.M., Konecini, V.J. & Novaco, R.W. 1984, *Aggression in Childhood and Youth*, Nijhoff Publishing, The Hague.

Knight, B.A. 1992, 'The roles of the student in mainstreaming', *Support for Learning*, vol. 7, no. 4, pp. 163–5.

Macoby, E.E. & Jacklin, C.N. 1974, *The Psychology of Sex Differences*, Stanford University Press, California.

Macoby, E.E. & Jacklin, C.N. 1980, 'Sex differences in aggression: a rejoinder and reprise', *Child Development*, no. 51, pp. 964–80.

McGrath, H. & Francey, S. 1993, *Friendly Kids, Friendly Classrooms*, Longman Cheshire, Melbourne.

Meichenbaum, D. 1977, *Cognitive Behaviour Modification*, Plenum Press, New York.

Morgan, D.P. & Jenson, W.R. 1988, *Teaching Behaviourally Disordered Students: Preferred Practices*, Merrill Pub. Co., Toronto.

Nelson, J. 1981, *Positive Discipline*, Ballantyne Books, New York.

Olweus, D. 1978, *Aggression in the Schools: Bullies and Whipping Boys*, Hemisphere, Washington DC.

Pikas, A. 1991, 'A pure concept of mobbing given the best results for treatment' in P.K. Smith & D. Thompson, *Practical Approaches to Bullying*, David Fulton, London.

Nabukoza, D. & Smith, P.K. 1992, 'Bullying in schools: mainstream and special needs', *Support for Learning*, vol. 7, no. 1, pp. 3–7.

Poteet, J.A. 1973, *Behaviour Modification: A Practical Guide for Teachers*, University of London Press, London.

Rigby, K. & Slee, R. 1993, *Bullying In Schools* (video recording and instruction manual), ACER, Hawthorn, Victoria.

Robertson, J. 1989, *Effective Classroom Control — Understanding Teacher–Pupil Relationships*, 2nd edn, Hodder & Stoughton, London.

Rogers, W. 1989, *Making a Discipline Plan*, Nelson, Melbourne.

Rogers, W. 1990, *You Know the Fair Rule*, ACER, Hawthorn, Victoria.

Rogers, W. 1991a, 'Attention-deficit disorder', *Behaviour Problems Bulletin*, vol. 5, no. 1, May, pp. 12–19.

Rogers, W. 1991b, 'Dealing with procrastination', **set** no. 1, ACER, Hawthorn, Victoria.

Rogers, W. 1992a, *Supporting Teachers in the Workplace*, Jacaranda Press, Queensland.

Rogers, W. 1992b, 'Early intervention programmes for behaviourally disordered students in mainstream school', in *Student Behaviour Problems: Directions, Perspectives and Expectations*, (eds) B. Willis & J. Izard, ACER, Hawthorn, Victoria.

Rogers, W. 1993a, 'The world of cue — non-verbal communication in the class-room', in *Student Behaviour Problems*, (eds) D. Evans, M. Myhill & J. Izard, ACER, Hawthorn, Victoria.

Rogers, W. 1993b, 'Taming bullies — a whole-school focus', *Classroom*, May, pp. 12–15.

Rogers, W. 1993c, *The Language of Discipline: A Practical Approach to Effective Class-room Management*, Northcote House, Plymouth.

Rosenthal, R. & Jacobsen, L.F. 1967, 'Teacher expectations for the disadvantaged', readings from *Scientific American*, W.F. Freeman & Co., San Francisco.

Rubin, K. & Pepler, D. (eds) 1991, *The Development and Treatment of Childhood Aggression*, Erlbaum, Hillsdale, New Jersey.

Rutter, M., Maughan B., Mortimore, P. & Ouston J. 1979, *Fifteen Thousand Hours*, Open Books, London.

Seligman, M. 1991, *Learned Optimism*, Random House, Sydney.

Serfontein, G. 1990, *The Hidden Handicap: How to Help Children who Suffer from Dyslexia, Hyperactivity and Learning Difficulties*, Simon & Schuster, Sydney.

Silberman, C.F. 1970, *Crisis in The Classroom*, Random House, New York.

Slee, P. 1992, Peer victimisation at school: you can run, but you can't hide, paper presented to the Behaviour Problems Conference, ANU, Canberra.

Smith, P. K. & Thompson, D. (eds) 1991, *Practical Approaches to Bullying*, David Fulton, London.

Stones, R. 1991, *No More Bullying*, Dinosaur Press (Harper Collins), London.

Van Houten, R. 1980, *Learning through Feedback*, Human Sciences Press, New York.

Wheldhall, K. (ed.) 1991, *Discipline in Schools: Psychological Perspectives on the Elton Report*, Routledge, London.

Wolpe, J. & Lazarus, A. 1966, *Behaviour Therapy Techniques*, Pergammon Press, Oxford.

Wragg, J. 1989, *Talk Sense to Yourself: A Program for Children and Adolescents*, ACER, Hawthorn, Victoria.